SANDPLAY THERAPY

TREATMENT OF PSYCHOPATHOLOGIES

Sandplay Therapy

Treatment of Psychopathologies

Edited by Eva Pattis Zoja

English translation by Henry Martin

DAIMON
VERLAG

English translation by Henry Martin, except for the essay by Lorenzo Bignamini, where the translation was provided by the author, and the essay by Ruth Ammann, which has been translated by Louise Mahdi.

ISBN 3-85630-622-6

Cover photo: see p. 247 for the description

for Lorenzo

Acknowledgments

to my teachers in sandplay therapy

to the authors, who have assumed the expense of the translation of their texts into English

to Henry Martin for his patience in correcting and adjusting the chaos of the different translations

to Ruth Ammann for kindly providing the cover photograph

to ISST for its encouragement

to Luigi Zoja for his decisive suggestions

A special thank you
to my Aunt, Marianne Stolz, who does not know anything about sandplay, but who rescued the whole project with her generous financial support just when it seemed to be irretrievably bogged down

Finally, with gratitude to all my family, who allowed so much of my time and energy to be devoted to this project

EVA PATTIS ZOJA

Contents

Color versions of all the pictures in this book can be viewed at
www.daimon.ch/Sandplay

Introduction

Eva Pattis Zoja

"How does one play with the sand?"

As she asks me this question, the patient begins to smile at herself. She realizes that prior to perceiving a new situation she is asking for rules. Knowing the rules of a game means understanding the possible requests that can come from the outside world. It makes no difference if the unconscious goal is to satisfy them, or to rebel against them: it's in any case a question of conforming automatically to an "external" situation before having shaped within oneself a feeling of one's own that might then enter into dialog with the outside world.

"The thing that most disturbs me when I find myself in front of the sandbox," another person remarks, "is the lack of criteria. I don't know what I'm supposed to do, or how I'm supposed to do it, or even if I have to do anything at all. There's a total lack of co-ordinates for how I'm supposed to be. Is it right to smooth out the surface of the sand, or would making a mountain be a better thing to do? Do I have to say something, or stay quiet? For the very first time I do not know what's being asked of me, and I don't have any tools for finding out. I feel as though I'm going under."

This book presents a theoretical and clinical description of sandplay therapy, as seen and practiced by ten European sandplay therapists. All of them discovered this particular field in the course of long and complex careers as practicing psychoanalysts, and in several cases after years of experience as psychiatrists and neuropsychiatrists. Francesco Montecchi is Director of the Department of Child Neuropsychiatry at Italy's most important children's hospital, "Ospedale Bambin Gesù," in Rome, and has to numbered, along with Stefano Marinucci and Andreina Navone, as one of the country's ground-breaking pioneers: for years, now, sandplay therapy has been employed as an official form of therapy for children at "Ospedale Bambin Gesù." Vito La Spina and Lorenzo Bignamini, members of the following generation, successfully continued similar work with both young adults and mature patients in their roles as Directors of departments of psychiatry at public clinics in Alghero and Milan.

All of the authors are Jungian analysts, with the exception of Marcella Merlino, and all except for Franco Castellana are members of the ISST, the International Society for Sandplay Therapy. Ruth Ammann, from Switzerland and a founding member of the Swiss Sandplay Association, is currently the President of the ISST, and her work on sandplay therapy and psychosomatics is well known throughout Europe.

Though the range of application for sandplay therapy has considerably widened in the course of the last few decades, especially in the United States, language barriers have continued to result in inadequate publication of theoretical work in sandplay therapy. It's to be hoped this book will be only the beginning of the publication of a vast body of work, to be shared internationally, on a variety of important topics.

The theoretical underpinnings of the sandplay work described in this book are marked by a number of special features. One of them is the high degree of attention directed to the process of the transference and the countertransference. The therapist is constantly in contact with his or her own thoughts, emotions, and bodily sensations in order to perceive the patient's non-verbal and unconscious communications, to "filter" them, and finally, in the proper way and at the proper time, to give them back to the patient.

Sandplay is not universally employed in such a form, or on the basis of such premises, but the members of the ISST see it as their common basis. It is only in this way that sandplay therapy unfolds its full potential as a differentiated, psychotherapeutic instrument. The "inexpressible," or "what has never existed, and all the same been experienced" finds initial manifestation as cryptic shapes in sand. These shapes are accompanied by emotions. These emotions little by little assume the form of visual images, endowed with symbolic content. This symbolic content or "surplus meaning" leads by way of association to new relevant images – perhaps from the patient's biography, perhaps from humanity's stock of collective images – and these in turn become episodes of a narrative. The discovery of words then leads to the shaping of thoughts and concepts. Exercising patience and omitting no necessary passages, we re-embark with sandplay on the long route of the development of consciousness. If we follow it successfully, empty and traumatized places in the patient's personal history will be healed.

The pathologies which this book describes as open to successful treatment with sandplay therapy range from psychotic disturbances, to the borderline syndrome, addiction, the lesions left by child abuse, the psychosomatic illnesses, and character disturbances.

I hope this book will make it clear that working with sand is more than a technical operation. The confrontation between the ego and the unconscious can never be a question of mastering a technique, which, once learned, can be expected to guarantee certain results. The confrontation between the ego and the unconscious is a dramatic existential situation, of which the final outcome is always unpredictable: something which even a prophet could never foresee.

While this book was being prepared, a tragic event took place. In July of this year, Lorenzo Bignamini became the victim of a murderous paranoid delusion on the part of one his patients.

It's to Lorenzo, now, that we dedicate this book. His life bore witness to the various ways in which the constant confrontation between the ego and the unconscious is an act no less of courage than of generosity.

Understanding with the Hands

Eva Pattis Zoja

The ten year old Carl had a wooden ruler in his yellow pencil case, and he began one day to whittle on the end of it. Not that anything special was on his mind; he was simply doing it. He carved away, and the final result was "a little manikin, about two inches long, with frock coat, top hat, and shiny black boots." He colored the manikin black with ink, sawed him off the ruler and put him in the pencil case, where he made a little bed for him. He even made him a coat from a scrap of wool. Then he had the feeling that he needed something more. He took a stone from his pocket, painted it, and laid it in the pencil case. He remarked to himself, "That's his stone." He hid the pencil case with the manikin on one of the beams beneath the roof of the family house. He knew that no would discover his secret.

He was later to write in his memoirs, "In all difficult situations, whenever I had done something wrong or my feelings had been hurt ... I thought of my carefully bedded-down and wrapped-up manikin and his smooth, prettily colored stone."[1]

This was Carl's game at the "climax and conclusion" of his childhood. That manikin, two inches long, was capable of establishing inner order, when everything outside was falling apart.

What happened with the rest of the ruler is something we do not know.

Thirty years later, the psychiatrist Dr. Carl Gustav Jung discovered that similar manikins and similar painted stones were used by the Australian aborigines. His childhood game came back to mind,[2] and he experienced an insight which led to one of the foundations of his work: the discovery of the collective unconscious. Play lay at the roots of the discovery of his main ideas.

Jung also played quite often in later years. But he didn't think of it simply as "playing." He always asked himself the question, "Now, really, what are you about?"[3] The whole body of his theoretical work is an answer to that question.[4]

Dora Kalff seems likewise to have asked herself this question. This is clear from her descriptions of her thoughts during therapy sessions. She didn't find it necessary to give them any outside theoretical formulation.

But she invented something new. Jung had achieved perception of interior visual images by way of active imagination. In sandplay, perceived interior images can be expressed three-dimensionally. But this is what's new: in sandplay, there are times when the hands unconsciously give shape to a form. It's first given shape and afterwards perceived. This image thus enters consciousness not from the inside, but from the outside.

Psychic substance is materialized with the help of the hands; one can touch it. For a moment, psyche and matter can no longer be distinguished from one another. This was Dora Kalff's inspired intuition.

Dora Kalff made concrete use – even nearly concretistic use – of Jung's ideas. She wasn't content with imagination, and created conditions in which unconscious contents can be retrieved from matter itself. In terms of the history of consciousness, this counts as a regression. For a concrete object to be charged with psychic substance, for it not to be simply an image of something, but actually to "work" on its own as a *pars pro toto*, hearkens back to a very distant phase of human development.[5] It takes us back to the magical phase, in which magic wasn't yet performed through words, recitations and incantations, but through things to be touched and handled, through amulets made from parts of plants or animals, through tiny figures. Narrative, myth, and fable had not yet been invented. This period's representations of human beings often depict them without mouths.

Jean Gebser offers a thorough description of this phase of human development in his work *The Ever Present Origin*.[6] He distinguishes five phases of the history of consciousness: the archaic phase, the magical phase, the mythic phase, and the mental phase, which is the one in which we currently live. (He then describes a future, integrated phase of development, which we have yet to achieve.)

In each of these phases, the human being finds access to a new dimension. Each transition from one phase to the next also causes the values of the foregoing phase to be experienced as deficient. (Since the end of the magical phase, magic has consisted of nothing but tricks; starting with the close of the mythic phase, ever more narratives have been produced, but no longer have cathartic effects; the final years of the mental phase see an ever more imposing accumulation of rational knowledge, but it no longer holds any meaning.)

If we delve a bit further into these terms, it soon becomes clear that most of what Jung discusses – the search for a personal myth, the complexes as forgotten gods – relates to the mythic phase. This is the phase in which the human being has first grown capable of the conscious perception of images, and of transforming them into narrative.

Sandplay, on the other hand, isn't necessarily built on narrative and reaches further back. Its roots lie in the magical phase.

Whenever the transition from one phase to the next hasn't been fully mastered, there's a tendency to regress into the former phase. We can see this as an unconscious attempt to achieve an harmonious existence, a wholeness, on a lower level. In therapy we can make good use of such regressions, since the valuable thing about them is that they put us back in touch with abilities and modes of perception that came in the course of progress to be seen as inferior, and to be abandoned.

Play is an excellent example of this.

Sandplay now gives us the possibility not only of reaching very far back into the individual childhood, but also of regressing to analogous depths in mankind's collective childhood.

This is to say that our differentiated, mentally oriented, present-day ego goes back through Dora's time machine directly into the magical phase. Psyche and matter are still undifferentiated, so a miniature of a tree *is* a living tree; it's the very essence of "treeness." We entrust ourselves to this trance-like atmosphere in which objects are living things, and we allow it to guide us.

But we also know that experiments with time machines are dangerous. The machine may be defective, and one runs the risk of no longer being able (or of being only partly able) to return to the time in which one customarily lives. The worst part, moreover, is that the person in question doesn't even realize that such a thing has happened.

Dora Kalff herself didn't fall victim to this risk. But this has to do with her personality and not with sandplay. Sandplay runs the danger, more than other therapies, of leading to a regression, and of leaving things that way.

Dora Kalff was open to all the irrational impulses that approached her from the worlds of the past. She performed her experiments, but she always remained within the great theoretical framework of her predecessors: Freud and Jung.

Without Freud's discovery of psychoanalysis, neither Jung's approach to psychotherapy nor Dora Kalff's sandplay therapy would be thinkable. Freud invented the situation in which two people regularly meet each other, at the same time and place, with a view to excluding the usual forms of communication, and committing themselves, in a particular way, to unconscious phenomena, within a free and protected space. But then he filled the unconscious with interpretations which he then again excluded from it. He discovered a new continent, but described it from points of view that largely derive from the old natural sciences and their categories of cause and effect. Jung is the person we have to thank for the first breakthrough from the thinking of the natural sciences, and for entry into a spiritual dimension. One remembers that ruler — an instrument of precision and measurement — which his game transformed into a living manikin.

Dora Kalff, however — with the help of Jung's discoveries, her own spiritual instinct, and her own talent as a therapist — was to discover a way to preserve the "freedom" of the space which Freud discovered. Is that truly so important? I think it is.

If we attempt to lift Dora Kalff's invention of sandplay therapy out of this historical context, believing that it's capable of standing alone, we run the danger of doing nothing more than to simulate the final product of a process. Successfully achieved end products often look deceptively simple; one believes it possible to save oneself the trouble of the initial, preparatory steps from which they organically developed. Such simulations of end products appear in cultural history as "isms," in religion as sects, and in political life as catastrophes.

So, the forebears of sandplay therapy are found, on the one hand, in pre-scientific healing rituals which are thousands of years old, and, on the other hand, in psychoanalysis, which has existed for barely a century.

If we neglect these two forebears, sandplay loses its individuality, its special features. If its traditional dimension is neglected, we reduce it to a psychoanalytic technique; if its psychological side is neglected, the result is more problematic: in the absence of the framework of an analytical setting, and in the absence of patient work on the countertransference, the unconscious contents of the therapist and those of the patient come to be confused with one another. Therapist and patient become fascinated by the archetypal contents that sandplay constellates, and their appearance isn't followed by the slow integration of these contents into consciousness. They don't give rise to understanding. The question, "Now, really, what are you about?" remains unanswered. The patient intuits that something fundamental is missing, but cannot formulate it. As a good patient, he'll repress his aggression, and idealize sandplay. Just as there is a false self, there are also false processes. They look very similar to authentic ones, but tend never to reach an end. The patient has two routes by which to leave this blind alley: he either feels betrayal and anger and stops the process, or he identifies with it and becomes a training candidate for this form of sandplay.

But if both sides of sandplay – the traditional side and the modern side – are respected, it stands among the avant-gardes of the methods in psychic healing, and ranks as an extraordinary instrument.

Our modern, psychoanalytic way of healing has developed considerably in recent decades. Aside from Jung, authors such as Spitz, Mahler, Klein, Winnicott, Reich, Bion, Fairbarn, Bolwby and Stern have enormously refined and deepened our abilities for listening. Yet in spite of these theoretical achievements, the practice of psychoanalysis – inclusive of Jungian analysis – has limits. And these limits, for example, are clearly present whenever we encounter preverbal and presymbolic states. Through perception of the countertransference, the analyst, yes, has access to these regions of experience, and can understand them; but we nonetheless find it difficult to transform that understanding into language. This is because the language involved ought to be the patient's language, and not the analyst's language. And at these levels, the patient's language is only a body language. The patient finds it impossible to recount a preverbal experience, since the patient has no verbal memory of such an experience, and often has even no visual image that derives from it. Our earliest emotional experiences are recorded in the body only as muscular tensions, or as vegetative reactions. None of the theoretical psychoanalysts has also developed – in addition to theory – a means of expression that corresponds to these earliest phases of development. Sandplay, in this sense, is the only self-consistent form of therapy: it deals with preverbal and presymbolic areas of experience by way of the shaping and manipulation of concrete objects. The hands assume the leading role: the body assumes the leading role. Not narrative, not language. Sandplay follows the patient into his or her particular phase of development, and its flexibility is sufficiently great as to allow it completely to adapt itself to whatever the patient's current needs. It has the presence at times of raw matter, at others of form, at others of image, at others of words. So it's functional at all these levels: the bodily and pre-symbolic, the imaginative, the eidetic, the symbolic, and as well the verbal.

Now I'd like to offer an example that shows how modern psychoanalytic technique and traditional healing practices flow over into one another. Both the analyst and the shaman work with identification. The healer coalesces with the patient for a brief moment of time, as though seeing with the patient's eyes and hearing with the patient's ears: as though experiencing the patient from the inside. The analyst's subsequent step is to make the effort to integrate as much of this experience as possible into consciousness.

Here's the example:

A patient had been moving her hands through the sand for a considerable period of time. She seemed to be at ease, and she seemed to be searching for something. The analyst felt a sudden discomfort, nearly nausea. He concentrated on it, despite its being highly unpleasant, and attempted to feel his way into it. So, he was searching for a psychic correlative to this purely corporeal condition. He noted that the sensation of discomfort was accompanied by a strong feeling that "everything is hostile." He also noted that objects or forms with which he was well acquainted – like the pattern of the carpet in his office – had changed: festoons of flowers which always before had looked like festoons of flowers now suddenly looked like evil claws; even the carpet's usually pleasant colors screamed out and attacked each other. An entirely intolerable world. As he had grasped the feeling that "everything is hostile, the world is evil," his nausea had somewhat subsided. It seemed as though his bodily condition had already been transformed into psychic substance. Then came the thought, "the patient may have experienced a world or a state like this during the first days of her life." This thought was an hypothesis, an associative enrichment of the experience.

So, the analyst had started an interior digestive process. First he was gripped by a bodily experience. The patient had no consciousness of any such bodily experience; she had no memory of such a thing, and could therefore express it neither through words nor through images. It was a split-off fragment for which the only means of communication lay in being passed along to another body through an act of projective identification. It was a lost and aimlessly wandering piece of the soul. The analyst's body had now picked it up, since the analyst and the patient were sufficiently ready to let that happen.

The patient, whom the analyst at this particular moment asked how she felt, replied that she had never felt better, and now finally felt liberated.

And now? What does the analyst do? Does he keep this fragment? We've said that he performed an act of digestion. One could also say that he had resolved this wandering fragment into an image: but that was his image, not the patient's. What's to happen now? This still homeless "element" must somehow get back to the patient, and be recognized as her own, and integrated; otherwise, this whole interaction will come to nothing.

How should this come about?

A good interpretation would be a possibility. But not everybody has the talent for that. In the case I've described, the analyst found no convincing interpretation within himself. So, in the course of this session he said nothing. In the next session, a week later, the following took place:

At the beginning of the session, the patient felt disturbed by the analyst's presence. She said that he shouldn't look at what she was doing. After a while, she expressed surprise. She had drawn a line in the sand, and said: "Oh, look! That's death." The analyst looked at the sand and saw the face of an infant. Its mouth was open in a scream, its forehead seemed crushed. The image gave off a feeling of extreme desperation. The analyst said, "What I see looks more like a child." The patient was struck, and began to cry, and had a strong cathartic reaction.

"How," she asked, "could my mother not have seen this?" "This" referred to the child's desperation.

It seems as though the split-off experience of the previous sitting had now taken shape on its own, and shown itself in the sand. The patient had drawn nothing but lines in the sand, and this "materialized" scream – along with the child – had suddenly stood within it.

Starting out from these emotional experiences, it was slowly possible to work towards integration; the "intolerable" was represented step by step, and described. "Child" motifs could be seen in the sand, again and again. Only several months later did the face of a cautiously smiling child appear, among thick curls of hair.

Analysis, here, had begun its work in the realm of pre-symbolic representation. There had been no form, no image, no memory, nothing but a bodily sensation which had been transmitted to the body of the analyst.

The shaman too temporarily takes the patient's illness into his own body. Then a transformation of this thing that makes the patient sick takes place. And afterwards the shaman has all sorts of possibilities for once again getting rid of it.

The psychoanalyst first elaborates it for himself (in Bion's terms, he transforms "beta" elements into "alpha" elements) and then attempts an interpretation. In sandplay, on the other hand, the restitution takes place in the way that's most direct and logical. It passes once again through the body. That's to say that now it's up to the patient's body – the patient's hands – to reappropriate and shape in sand the piece of the soul which has been split off, and which the analyst has digested. Now the patient can see it in the sand. Since this bodily condition has become an image, it can find is way into consciousness, with the help of the analyst's work as a catalyst.

So, we find ourselves in the prescientific healing arts, and *also* in modern psychoanalysis. Projective identification is the most primitive form of communication, and as well the most refined of our analytical instruments. By means of it, even a variety of elements which are presymbolic, formless, and without access to images can be grasped, and then resolved into image.

Let's now draw a few more distinctions between sandplay and analysis without sand. I don't say "verbal analysis," since there is no such thing as entirely verbal analysis. Every effective interpretation comes into being on the basis of the analyst's non-verbal perceptions.

First of all, there is a structural difference: the triangular constellation of sandplay. In sandplay, the room no longer holds only two participants. Instead there are three: the client, the analyst, the sand. Three is an unstable number, and easily falls apart into two plus one. (As is surely clear to anyone who is one of three siblings.)

In the setting of analysis, two individuals attempt to elaborate a third region of communication, which is the symbolic dimension. Together they create a field of energy that's enriched with unconscious elements, and they attempt to grasp a few of them, and to bring them into consciousness. If they don't succeed, their shared unconscious will tend toward acting out.

Sandplay begins differently. This third and potentially symbolic space is foreseen and present from the start as something concrete and material. It is simply there.

In terms of the patient's attitude, this situation often causes a sudden constellation of its other, hidden side.

The analyst offers an additional, concrete space, which indeed is more neutral than the analyst might be. It invites the patient to communicate with him- or herself. There's a sense in which the patient is more alone with him- or herself. Everything that's painful, or that causes fear or rage, can now make its appearance. The analyst stands far less "in the way." And for the patient, everything bad is out there in the sand, and not inside the Self. The patient can temporarily distance from it, while nonetheless staying in touch with it.

For patients who constellate intense transferences, this also means that they have come into possession of a piece of the analyst, and can peacefully and quietly take control of it, without having to be afraid that the analyst may feel wounded, overwhelmed, or too intensely loved. Everything unimaginable can take place first in the sand, and only later be risk being voiced within the relationship.

Jung describes the transition from three (a dynamic number) to four in *Aion*. Whatever has remained excluded from a whole will be drawn into play by the triangular situation's instability.

Even before anything has been expressed in the sand, this triangular situation can also activate the most primitive tendencies toward the splitting of the personality.

We normally presuppose that unconscious contents allow themselves to be given three-dimensional representation in sandplay. But this holds true for contents which are close to consciousness, and which already exist in the form of images. But there are also unconscious elements which have no form at all, and no connection with images; they may even, perhaps, as yet possess no psychic substance. In dreams too they don't present themselves as images, but instead can be considered the underlying structure of certain dreams: invisible but omnipresent, and omni-determinant. Such elements show the tendency to explode all frameworks. So, they can be neither remembered nor represented. But they constantly constellate themselves in relationships.

The triangular sandplay situation makes itself available to precisely such invisible "disruptive" elements, and we then find the following sort of scene:

In one session, the patient plays with the sand and is full of initiative. He experiences the sand as pleasant, shapeable, protective, and he feels at ease. "If only," he thinks, "the analyst weren't there, disturbing things by scribbling away in his notebook. He blocks my creativity. He controls my movements. If he weren't there, I could make all sorts of things...."

At the next session, the same patient begins by declaring that the sand feels cold and coarse. Its color too strikes him as different; it's darker. What's happened? Nothing at all seems to want to take shape. And the miniatures? They had always seemed so inviting. But now they just stand around and look so ridiculous, pure kitsch. Luckily the analyst is there. He sits there patiently. He's someone at least you can talk to. He'll understand.

On one occasion the sand is good and the analyst is bad. The next time around the sand is bad and the analyst is good. The patient has the personal experience, through all his senses, that the same sand and the same analyst repeatedly flip-flop, and reverse their qualities. This is to say that the patient can catch his own unconscious splitting phenomena while in fact they're underway. The analyst had done nothing to promote that awareness, and simply allows himself to be used as a neutral object. In this particular moment, he too was one of the miniatures, and the sandbox was the whole room, the whole analytical setting.

The triangular situation not only gives patients an additional realm of expression; it also does the same for the analyst.

Since the patient is only partially focused on the analyst, the analyst too has a greater chance to constellate an "other side." He sees what the patient creates in the sand, and at the very same time has an interior perception of it, as though looking into *his own* imaginative sandbox. He perceives his thoughts, his feelings, his bodily sensations, his impulses to say or do something, and all of these things can be reactions to what's taking place in the sand. He then elaborates these perceptions internally, without directly communicating them. He's involved in something like digesting them, before attempting to give them back to the patient. Yet, giving them back may often not even be necessary, since what the analyst has meanwhile processed may appear in the sand on its own.

Let's now move on to the last of the differences which we are able here to discuss between sandplay and analysis without sand. The hands.

As Ruth Amman remarks, the hands pick up a movement that comes from the body, and they allow themselves to be guided by it. The existence of a level of bodily perception that doesn't pass through consciousness has today been confirmed by research in neurophysiology. Damasio offers an example.[7] Patients who suffer from visual agnosia are unable to recognize photographs of relatives since particular regions of their brains have been damaged. They look at such a photo and remark that they have never seen that person before. But their bodies react to the image. There are highly significant changes in the electrical resistance of the skin, and also in body temperature. The body "recognizes" the photo, without any participation from consciousness.

So, the hands are vehicles not only of unconscious self-expression, but can also perceive a feeling, an atmosphere, an interactive field without these things having passed through a process of consciousness.

In the early stages of child development, the hands and the mouth are linked to one another. The sucking reflex and the reflex of closing the fists can both be observed within the uterus.

While nursing, babies often close and open their fists in accord with their sucking rhythm. During these first few weeks and months, emotional experience takes place in the region of the mouth (in the "oral cavity," as R. Spitz[8] calls it) and is accompanied by the gestures of the hands. The ways in which some patients handle the sand can be quite reminiscent of these movements on the part of infants.

The possible existence of a special bond between a patient's mouth and hands once presented itself before my mind on hearing the woman remark: "Words are different when my hands are in the sand." She had always gotten lost within her words, ceaselessly talking away and growing ever more confused. Since starting to sit before the sand, she had begun to speak differently. She spoke more slowly; she made pauses; she repeated words and sentences; her speaking took on a rhythm. Above all, she now for the very first time patiently listened to herself.

Contact between the sand and the palms of the hands will sometimes activate a patient's earliest experiences.

An example.

The patient moved the sand, and said it was like the sea. This continued for a while, and she felt at ease. Then she had the feeling that the sea was sucking her under; she felt dizzy; it was "sucking out her brain."

A state of disintegration had come to expression as both an image and a bodily sensation.

Now she gripped the sand tightly in her fists, and remarked that the undertow and the dizziness had ceased. She was relieved. She began again to open her hands and to feel the sea, and the terrifying undertow returned. Again she closed her fists around the sand.

She had the crucial experience that she herself could put an end to the undertow; that by tightly holding the sand, she could also hold onto herself. Concretely holding onto the sand thus turned into holding herself psychically together. The remembered condition of disintegration was now counterbalanced by a new experience: that now this state – unlike before – could be halted by an act of will. Having an effect on the outside world is one of a small child's most important experiences, since it's by way of such experiences that the formation of the ego takes place.

In conclusion, now, I'd like to offer a few more words on the naming of things, and on the liberation that can come through language.

When words are spoken at the right moment, they can be just as vital as miniatures, and there are cases in which they assume such functions: they serve as the analyst's miniatures.

If sandplay remains exclusively preverbal, the final step – the step that brings us into the present – remains unachieved.

The orientation of the world in which we live is mental. In order to be able to understand it, and not simply to live in it passively, we must speak its language, which is to say that *we* have to be able to coordinate our thoughts, ideas and images by way of words.

We cannot behave as though we did not have our present-day ego – our complicated, verbally-oriented ego – simply because there are times when it causes us to suffer.

When I began to see Dora Kalff for sessions, I had worked as a Jungian analyst for eight years. I knew I could learn sandplay from her, but I wasn't expecting to learn much from what she'd *say*.

In one session, I picked up a handful of sand, and let it run slowly down like rain, all over everything, for a good deal of time. It gave off a barely audible rustle. I found this event quite wonderful, and it was more than enough for me. But then came the point, after quite some time had passed, when Dora Kalff carefully brought her words into this silent event: "And that's how every tiniest grain of sand finds its place." These unrequested words changed something fundamental.

Her words were no explanation, and no interpretation. But they delineated a meaning. Without these words, this experience, once the session was over, would have slipped back into unconsciousness, and would probably have succumbed in the world of everyday reality. It was by way of Dora Kalff's words that it became a part of my life.

So, sandplay can be just as verbal as every good analysis.

Its special feature lies in its quantum-like readiness in any given moment to jump from matter to psyche, or from psyche to matter. It is always just as much matter as needed, and just as much psyche as possible; or just as much matter as possible, and just as much psyche as needed.

References

1 Jung, C. G. (1972), *Memories, Dreams, Reflections,* recorded and edited by Aniela Jaffé, London and Glasgow: Collins, The Fontana Library, Random House, p. 37.
2 Ibid., p. 38, "There came to me, for the first time, the conviction that there are archaic psychic components which have entered the individual psyche without any direct line of tradition."
3 Ibid., p. 197.
4 Ibid., p. 225, "It all began then; the later details are only supplements and clarifications of the material that burst forth from the unconscious, and at first swamped me. It was the *prima materia* for a lifetime's work."
5 Gebser, J. (1986), *The Ever Present Origin*, Athens: Ohio University Press.
6 Ibid.
7 Damasio, Antonio (1999), *The Feeling of What Happens, Body and Emotion in the Making of Consciousness*, New York: Harcourt.
8 Spitz, R. (1965), The First Year of Life: A Psychoanalytic Study of Normal and Deviant Development of Object Relations," New York: International Universities Press.

Sandplay Therapy in the Treatment of Borderline Personality Disturbance

Vito La Spina

> *In nova fert animus mutatas dicere formas*
> *corpora; di, coeptis (nam vos mutastis et illas)*
> *adspirate meis primaque ab origine mundi*
> *ad mea perpetuum deducite tempora carmen!*
>
> Of bodies chang'd to various forms, I sing:
> Ye Gods, from whom these miracles did spring,
> Inspire my numbers with coelestial heat;
> 'Till I my long laborious work compleat:
> And add perpetual tenour to my rhimes,
> Deduc'd from Nature's birth, to Caesar's times.
> — Ovid, *Metamorphoses*, I, 1-4

Humanistic thought puts *becoming* at the center of human experience, thus turning its attention not to *being*, but to *existence* in a world of time and change.

Before discussing a number of the pertinent applications of sandplay therapy as a psychoanalytic technique in the treatment

of Borderline Personality Disturbance (BPD), I'd like to note a few of the metamorphoses of:
- psychopathology
- the conceptual models of appropriate treatment
- the patient/therapist dyad.

Pathomorphosis

The interior world, the microcosm, exists in correlation with the outside world, the macrocosm, and this correlation finds expression in the constant shifts that come about in oneiric and psychopathological themes. Among patients with visual hallucinations, demons and gods have been transformed into flying saucers (Jung 1958); in delusions, the forces accused of inserting or stealing thoughts are ever less identified as witches and magicians, and ever more as television sets and laser beams; in dreams, the image of the horse is ever more frequently supplanted by the image of the motorcycle.

These changes inevitably reverberate through all the psyche's manifestations, both adaptive and pathological. So, they are also found in the mental illnesses, in the theoretical models that deal with them, and again in the roles and modes of communication that govern the inter-relationships of patients and therapists. In the second half of the nineteenth century, "hysteria" – which today's standard diagnostic systems ICD-10 (1992) and DSM-IV (1995) have meanwhile ceased to classify as a discreet and separate entity – was the mental disturbance most frequently *represented*. Between 1920 and 1990, it lost that distinction to the "idiopathic psychoses," which exerted so great a fascination on the psychiatric community as to induce the creation of the nosographic category of "schizophrenia," on the basis of the theoretical premise – which some were later to see as unfounded, artificial and arbitrary (Boyle 1990; Maj 1998) – "of the substantially identical course of various psychiatric syndromes previously considered to be separate entities." (Rossi Monti and Stanghellini 1999)

More recently, one notes the growing frequency of BPD, already defined in the classical period as "pseudoneurotic schizophrenia" (Hoch and Polatin 1949), but currently relegated by DSM-IV to the illnesses listed in Axis II. All the same, it has now become a kind of psychiatric trash bin, too frequently and poorly used. Patients in situations of diagnostic confusion can be labeled "borderline" for lack of anything better. (Gabbard 1994, p. 421)

Shifts in the Conceptual Models of Treatment

The ample availability of psychiatric drugs (antianxiety drugs, antidepressants, antipsychotics, tranquilizers, all of which now show fewer side effects than their predecessors) currently induces psychiatrists, as well as patients and their families, to think of drug treatment as the cornerstone of every therapy. Now, I don't intend in any way to deny or diminish the usefulness of pharmacological treatments: drugs are highly useful tools, and are often indispensable for successful therapeutic results. When necessary, I present them in the following terms to those of my patients who even while needing need them are afraid of growing dependent upon them: "You see," I tell them, "I myself am so nearsighted that without my glasses I wouldn't be able to recognize your face. I truly need my glasses in order to be able to see with sufficient clarity. And when I wake up in the morning, it surely doesn't cross my mind that I'm dependent on my glasses. I think, instead, that I am lucky to live in the present day and age. If I had lived a thousand years ago, I wouldn't have been able to do very much. I am just that nearsighted. Now, drugs are just like eyeglasses: they are tools that allow us to see the world more clearly."

But the fact that psychiatric drugs are frequently *necessary* doesn't imply that on their own they're *sufficient* for a cure. Quite the opposite. If drugs are not flanked by adequate psychotherapy, they can turn into cages (of habits, of rituals) that are very hard to get out of. In cases like that, a patient will need a drug for many years, even for decades. There are even times when patients turn their drugs into one of the symptoms of the disturbance they would like to treat. All the same, so long as both therapist and patient see their use as transitional, "psychiatric drugs don't necessarily represent the intrusion of a non-human object into the [doctor-patient] relationship." (Searles 1976, p. 404) The drug is prescribed by a doctor (not always a psychiatrist) for a patient (who can accept it, refuse it, or negotiate it) who lives in a particular social and family environment. The drug's administration is a scene in which doctor, patient and environment all interact in highly complex ways, as also influenced by the nature of the specific pathology (Nivoli 2001). In the case of BPD, for example, the patient may unconsciously use the drug as a mother substitute, or as a tool for acting out aggressiveness towards the psychiatrist or the environment, or as a way of finding relief from experiences of separation. But this is also to be seen, to some degree, as inherent to the situation, and constitutes a part of the patient's *work*: it's something that the therapist has to grasp, effectively to symbolize, and to interpret in ways that benefit the patient. Unfortunately, however, the doctor too can be dominated, in a drug's administration, by unconscious factors, which at times can be collusive, at times oppositional with respect to the patient or the environment. (See Clarkin, Yeomans and Kernberg 1999.) The doctor-patient relationship is by nature so intense as inevitably to set up complex webs of transference and countertransference, with possible violations of the setting. The Hippocratic oath, moreover, is proof that this phenomenon has been known since antiquity. Even the "biological" psychiatrists can run afoul of the "slippery slope" described by Gabbard and Lester (1995), especially with patients afflicted with BPD.

So, the possibilities offered by psychiatric drugs don't reduce but increase the importance of psychotherapy, and of adequate training on the part of the psychotherapist. In other words, making use of a metaphor that typifies our times, let's consider the computer: proper work on software can often solve problems with hardware, and even problems of a certain gravity. And aside from all questions of the differences between various programming languages, it's clear that it's at least to be hoped that the knowledge and competence of any technician who tinkers with software is both adequate and *certified*; the concrete ways in which such knowledge and competence will be put to use will in any case depend on the programmer's personality and on the nature of the hardware involved. There can be no doubt that:

- a computer can be programmed (or de-programmed) by an incompetent dabbler;
- a Ferrari can be started and driven by an amateur, and even by a person without a driving license;
- an analysis can be conducted by a non-analyst.

But it's also clear that all three cases are open to unpredictable results.

On the other hand, the psychiatric literature of the last twenty years reports on interventions that distance ever more from the psychoanalytic model, thanks as well to the pressures exerted by insurance companies in favor of less expensive treatments. (Loriedo 2002, p. 8) The widespread adoption of different models (which might crudely be defined, on the one hand, as primarily systematic and, on the other, as cognitive-behaviorist) has led many authors, including analysts, to theorize the *crisis of psychoanalysis*. Even while making no attempt to approach the field's specific epistemology, I'd nonetheless see it as more correct to speak of a *crisis of the models of the use of psychoanalysis*, largely owing to the scarce availability for researchers, especially at universities, of adequately trained therapists, and of research protocols suited to the analytic method. One might also speak, above all, of a *crisis of the psychoanalytic societies*, which are frequently established more for the gratification of personal needs (of recognition, of power) than for signaling and defending real and fundamental conceptual differences. (Ellenberger 1970) If they hope to survive – even before all question of maintaining scientific credibility – the psychoanalytic societies can no longer continue to avoid a confrontation with the EBM (Evidence Based Medicine) criteria adopted by the international scientific community (Gabbard 2001). Things, however, stand somewhat differently for the individual analysts, whose abilities and professional success depend no more than partly on the associations to which they belong.

But in this case: what sorts of psychotherapy (what sorts of therapists) are needed? What's shared by the treatments conducted by Freud, Jung and the other pioneers (treatments that lasted a matter of months) and those conducted by their followers (treatments that last for years, if not for decades)? Do the latter reflect the characteristics ("pre-Oedipic" rather than "Oedipic") of the patient? Or, instead, are they symptomatic of a pervasive (and "pre-Oedipic") "need for purity" on the part of the analyst? (Grunberger 1989)

Shifts in the Patient/Therapist Dyad

About half a century ago, Jung reached the conclusion that the passage from the age of Pisces to the age of Aquarius would go hand in hand with the manifestation of significant "changes in the constellation of the psychic dominants, of the archetypes, and of the 'gods,'" along with the progressive devitalization of the symbols that stem from our religious and cultural traditions. He felt that the archetypal theme of the hostile brothers (Cain and Abel, Romulus and Remus, etc.) would have to give way to that of the union of opposites, thus continuing the process of the differentiation of consciousness. (Jung 1951; Jung 1958; Colonna 2000) But the widespread dominance of rational/instrumental thought that characterizes the global market of contemporary technological society has produced an extraordinary abundance of images ("media, electronic, virtual, and advertising images, not psychic images" – photography, cinema, television, the internet) which transforms knowledge into the "mass transmission of information" and, even more, into "concrete visual act." The result is that opposites have come to be *superimposed*, without being unified. And since the visual image has assumed ascendancy over both the object and its psychic image, symbolic activity comes to be hampered. We have thus seen the start of a dangerous process of "depsychologization and disanimazation" (Panepucci 2000, p. 43) which reduces – and sometimes calls to a halt – the activation of the special psychic resource to which Jung (1958) referred as the *transcendent function*, and without which the analytic field (which consists of the patient and the analyst) is condemned to the sterility of an endless present.

> If all time is eternally present
> All time is unredeemable
>> – T. S. Eliot, "Four Quartets," I, 4-5

Among the many consequences, one also notes the spread of a mother complex which at the collective level finds expression as a demand for comfort and entitlement. At the analytic level, it tends to shift the patient/analyst dyad from the paradigm of father/son (which characterized the well-delimited analytic territories of the founders) to that of mother/child (which is generally typical of the scumbled horizons of their followers).

> *Iamque mare et tellus nullum discrimen habebant:*
> *omnia pontus erat, derant quoque litora ponto.*

> Now seas and Earth were in confusion lost;
> A world of waters, and without a coast.

> — Ovid, *Metamorphoses*, I, vv. 291-292

Excessive importance of the visual image impairs the transcendent function. From the clinical point of view, this in turn induces the pathomorphosis that leads from hysteria (where displacement is the ego's defense mechanism) to schizophrenia (where defenses take the form of fragmentation) and then to BPD, which is characterized by *rapid oscillations between irreconcilable opposites* (the defense mechanisms are devaluation/idealization and, above all, splitting and projective identification).

Borderline Personality Disturbance

BPD is the mental illness that more than any other, today, reflects the spirit of the times: it recreates in the interior world the inhibition of symbolic activity that afflicts the outside world. (See Gullotta 2001) Instead of the union (*unio oppositorum*) one has a superimposition of opposites (*superpositio oppositorum*) which remain non-integrated and split off, in the timeless world of an endless present.

BPD can be diagnosed, as specified by DSM-IV, in the presence of:

"A pervasive pattern of instability of interpersonal relationships, self-image, and affects, and marked impulsivity, beginning by early adulthood and present in a variety of contexts, as indicated by five (or more) of the following:

1) frantic efforts to avoid a real or imaginary abandonment.
Note: This does not include the suicidal or self-mutilating forms of behavior considered under criterion 5.

2) a pattern of unstable and intense interpersonal relations characterized by alternating between extremes of idealization and devaluation.

3) identity disturbance: markedly and persistently unstable self-image or sense of self.

4) impulsivity in at least two areas that are potentially self-damaging (e.g., spending, sex, substance use, reckless driving, binge eating).
Note: Does not include suicidal or self-mutilating behavior covered in Criterion 5.

5) recurrent suicidal behavior, gestures, or threats, or self-mutilating behavior.

6) affective instability due to a marked reactivity of mood (e.g. intense episodes of dysphoria, irritability or anxiety, usually lasting a few hours, and only rarely more than a few days).

7) chronic feelings of emptiness.

8) inappropriate, intense anger, or difficulty controlling anger (e.g., frequent displays of temper, constant anger, recurrent physical fights).

9) transient, stress-related paranoid ideation, or severe dissociative symptoms."

The ICD-10 refers to BPD as "Disturbance of the emotionally unstable, borderline type personality." And after this affirmation of the crucial importance for diagnostic purposes of affective instability, ICD-10 goes on to remark that the borderline type is characterized by:

"a marked tendency to act impulsively without consideration of the consequences, along with affective instability. The ability to formulate projects for the future is minimal, and fits of intense rage can frequently lead to violence or 'explosive behavior.' Such episodes are easily triggered when impulsive actions are criticized or impeded by others."

And with specific reference to the "Disturbance of the emotionally unstable, borderline type personality," the affliction shows:

"various characteristics of emotional instability; and the subject's self-image, the goals the subject pursues, and the subject's personal preferences (inclusive of sexual preferences) are often disturbed or unclear. Constant feelings of interior emptiness are usually present. The tendency to be involved in intense and unstable relationships can trigger repeated emotional crises and be associated with excessive efforts to avoid abandonment, as well as with series of suicide attempts or acts of self-mutilation (even though these can also occur without apparent triggering events)."

BPD occurs in about 2% of the general population, and is diagnosed in 10-20% of the clinical population. About 75% of the persons affected are women.

The illness appears in late adolescence or early adulthood. Its course, even though highly variable, is generally more grave in earlier years, less grave in adulthood, and after the age of forty it tends to stabilize or resolve itself (see DSM-IV, p. 712). It has been shown that there is an overlap, on the order of about 69%, between Major Depressive Disturbance and BPD, and that 3-10% of the patients who suffer from BPD commit suicide.

It is my opinion that BPD and the psychological phenomena that determine and characterize it (with particular reference to emotional resonance/projective identification, as well as to splitting …) don't exclusively appear among human beings, but are also found in various forms among the other mammals. The observation of animal behavior has been amply employed in psychopharmacological research. (Gessa and Serra 1990)

While making no claims for its ethological validity, I'd like to present an observation.

D is a pre-adolescent of English origins whose parents were members of a minor, rural nobility, and forced into a union by powerful family conditionings, based on motives of interest.

From the time of D's early infancy, specifically economic factors led to his being entrusted to three different families. His failure, however, to satisfy the expectations of his foster families, and especially of their heads of family, always led to his being returned to his family of origin, where he continued to wait for a definitive placement that grew ever more difficult to realize, given a number of his modes of behavior which others perceived as highly disturbing. If left alone, D. experienced episodes of intense anxiety, howling out of desperation with such intensity as to the excite the reactions of neighbors; he damaged household furniture and bric-a-brac to the point of panto-clasticism, even while never turning his aggressiveness directly against the persons with whom he lived; he showed intense phobic reactions to sudden noise, and constantly attempted to run away from home. He tends as well, in moments of emotional excitement, to lose control of his sphincters.

In December 2001, D. was assigned to a fourth foster family (composed of a father, a mother, a ten year old son, and three other relatives of more than eighty years of age), which initially had been interested only in adopting an infant. Their encounter with D., however, had excited within them a particular affection for him, and they received him into an upper middle-class milieu that prized rationality more than emotivity and that lent particular attention to the respect of appearances and proper behavior. The father and mother were absent most of the time, given their professional responsibilities, as well as their active social life. Material prosperity was abundant, whereas the time the parents could dedicate to children was scarce. And D., precisely, was primarily in need of time. In the family fantasies, D. seemed destined to replace the "unforgettable" S., an adoptive daughter of Scottish origins, who some years previously had died precociously. S. was constantly held up to D. as an unattainable model, and he was often addressed, "by error," with her name. Here too, he acted out his symptomatic behavior patterns, in an escalation that culminated, shortly before Christmas, in a flight from the family home that lasted throughout the night. The foster parents initially searched for him without excessive zeal, next considered the possibility of giving him up and returning him to his family of origin, and finally reaccepted him – discovering themselves to be "strangely moved" – when he was brought back home by a collaborator who by chance had found him on the following morning as he wandered through the streets, confused, in disarray, and cold.

During the Christmas vacations, the parents could spend more time with their children. D. seemed progressively to adjust to the family, and to find a place within it. All the same, considerable failings in comportment persisted, such as to lead the foster family to leave him at home, alone, on the closing night of the year. When they returned to their home after a gala dinner and a fireworks display, they couldn't find him in the house. They excitedly sought for him everywhere, but could find no trace of him. Nearly an hour had passed before they discovered that D. had fallen from the terrace: a fall of some twenty-five feet. He had four fractured ribs, had difficulty breathing, and was nearly frozen.

While coming to his aid, the members of the foster family felt intense, conflicting emotions of relief and affliction. In the following days, D's health returned quite rapidly from a physical point of view, whereas his separation anxiety improved only slightly.

"D" is a year-old beagle who is useless for hunting; "S" was a Scotch terrier; the "foster family" is my own.

BPD is sometimes masked by apparently neurotic symptoms: for example, many such patients tell me in the course of their first visit that they're subject to "panic attacks." They've been given that definition by some television program, by a popular magazine, by the personnel at the first-aid station where they went to ask for help. I have had occasion, however, to note that if patients are allowed the time to describe what in fact they feel, "panic" proves to be a very general label, and what rises up from behind it is rage, emotional instability, feelings of emptiness and desperation, and those "intense episodes of dysphoria, irritability or anxiety" which appear in the diagnostic criteria of DSM-IV. So, the symptom of "panic" is effectively an expression of the *urgency* of the patient's demands: the patient knows no future (there can be no waiting or postponement), and has no past (there are no consoling memories). What the patient needs is needed here and now.

This sense of urgency is often transmitted to the therapist not only verbally but also emotionally. And if the countertransference is insufficiently elaborated, it can lead the therapist to varying forms of *acting out*, from prescribing or saying *too much*, to more serious violations of the setting. This takes place in the presence of a particular defensive use of an emotional *resonance* to which Klein refers as "projective identification"[1] (Migliorati 2001), and to which the dyad of patient and therapist is specifically susceptible.

If it is true that the desires of the patient afflicted with BPD demand immediate satisfaction, it is also true that their gratification is always and only illusory: it disappears no sooner than achieved, since the object sought lies outside the patient's sense of time and field of awareness. It leaves behind a desperate feeling of emptiness. When, on the other hand, gratification doesn't take place, idealization of the object desired (it makes no difference if internal or external) flip-flops into its devaluation; and splitting – producing objects which are all good or all bad, without intermediate colorations – will meanwhile hold in check the patient's psychotic elements. In significant interpersonal relationships, the patient afflicted with BPD continually attempts to circumvent the *conditional* acceptance that's typical of relations between adults (the condition is a question of respecting the terms of a personal contract), in order to revert to the *unconditional* acceptance which typifies the mother/child relationship. Even in the therapeutic relationship, the patient tends toward strategies of behavior that allow him or her to violate, or that stimulate others (the general environment, friends, relatives, the therapist) to violate contractually established limits.

So, the patient/analyst contract has to be clearly formulated, and the "therapeutic framework" (Clarkin, Yeomans and Kernberg 1995, p. 61) has to be meticulously protected. There is no other way to establish and maintain that condition of "the analyst's credibility" which is fundamental for therapy: "Since the patients never experienced such a form of credibility during the childhood period of maternal care, they have to start out by finding it for the very first time in the behavior of the analyst." (Winnicott 1965, p. 43)

In pathogenic terms, the most serious forms of BPD can be correlated to a deficit in the hallucinatory ability of the child, at a stage so precocious as to block or greatly to reduce the development of the faculty of symbolization (Freud 1911, pp. 455-6; Winnicott 1965). As well, according to the well-known Kernberg model (1992), BPD seems typically to relate to a crisis in development during the sub-phase of reapproach (in the sixteenth to the thirtieth month of life) of the phase of separation-individuation described by Mahler (1975). This crisis leads the individual to see their attempts to separate from the mother as endowed with the power to bring about her disappearance, thus making the subject incapable of tolerating solitude, and likewise apprehensive of every possibility of being abandoned by significant figures. Stability in the perception of the object is insufficient, and the subject never learns to integrate good and bad images, either of the Self or of the other, and they thus remain split and unrepresentable *at one and the same time.*

Sandplay Therapy in the Treatment of BPD

The difficulty experienced by the individual patient afflicted with BPD in achieving conscious awareness of the complexity of the emotions and images which present themselves as split is also aggravated by our culture's collective poverty in the field of symbolism. This tends to make it difficult to deploy analysis in the treatment of patients afflicted with BPD, and advises the use – flanked by treatment with psychiatric drugs – of the analytic techniques which most allow the activation of symbolization, and, through it, the process of the integration of opposites, as performed by the transcendent function.

Among them, a special role can be attributed to sandplay therapy, which allows the representation of the internal world on the very same terms in which it finds itself constellated: it has the power to offer visibility and re-cognizability to highly non-integratable or destructuring unconscious contents. Sandplay can furnish a possible language also to those who have no words through which to express their suffering (Montecchi 1993, p. 24; Montecchi 2000, p. XIV; Ammann 1989, pp. 10-11). In the method described by Kalff (1966) and Montecchi (1993), the therapist elaborates a structural and/or content-based interpretation of the patient's sand construction, but usually refrains from communicating it ("silent interpretation").

In sandplay therapy, the accentuated manifestation of the models of mental functioning which are typical of the primary process (Freud 1911) involve the analyst no less than the patient, according to the well-known "alchemical" model proposed by Jung (1946, p. 228):

Jung saw these levels of communication as forms of *parte-cipation mystique*; and the metaphors he chose to apply to their possibly uncontrolled transference/countertransference inter-actions were "emotional contagion," "personal contamination," and "psychic infection" (1935, pp. 57, 148).

Concerning the means that makes such forms of communi-cation possible, even in the case of silent interpretation (which, as I see it, is the true motor of sandplay therapy), it seems to me to be useful to return to the concept of the *psychoid* process (Jung 1947-1954, pp. 195-196) or of that intermediate *quid* between psyche and matter which it's possible to reach and to influence from both within and outside the body by way of certain forms of meditation: "this takes place since the human soul is not imprisoned by matter, but, quite the contrary, governs it" (von Franz 1988, pp. 144-145).

So, sandplay therapy constitutes a specific analytical instrument, and it can be used correctly only by expert analysts who have been adequately trained and who are capable of handling the complex problems of transference and countertransference that result from the activation within the patient/therapist dyad of pre- and non-verbal levels of communication which present themselves as among the most profound. The analyst's silent interpretations have the function of imparting order, and without them it seems quite likely that the images produced in the sandbox would remain no more than simple signs, without setting off a process of symbolization: the transcendent function would remain inhibited, the images created in sand would exacerbate mechanisms of splitting and activate dangerous processes of fragmentation, and their effects on the patient/therapist dyad would be uncontrolled and uncontrollable (see Jung 1935, p. 148).

A Clinical Example

Even in cases of BPD, the images constructed in the sandbox immediately reveal the defense mechanisms which are most employed by the patient's ego. With this in mind, I'd like to discuss a few of the constructions of one of my female patients.

Since a full clinical case study would extend beyond this article's goals, our comments here will limit themselves to the formal aspects of the images, thus ignoring a certain number of themes which are recognized as fundamental to effective therapy, since they bear directly on the transference, the countertransference (Sedgwick 1995) and symbols. The ways in which themes like these emerge into the analytic field – no less than the possibilities for grasping and understanding them – must always be seen in the light of the psychological types *of both patient and analyst*: "Last but not least [psychological typology] is an essential means for determining the 'personal equation' of the practicing psychologist, who, armed with an exact knowledge of his differentiated and inferior functions, can avoid many serious blunders in dealing with his patients." (Jung 1921, p. 555)

F. is a young woman, twenty-three years old, an only child, a university student. Her childhood was marked by *witnessing* the constant quarrels of her parents, as well as her mother's considerable sexual promiscuity. Her mother was also an alcoholic. At five or six years of age, one evening when her father was away at work, F. was alarmed by unusual noises that led her to try to make her way to her mother's bed-room. In the hall she saw an unknown man who fled as soon as he realized that he was being observed. She screamed and asked her mother for an explanation. Her mother replied. "It's nothing. You didn't see anything." From that point on, her relationship with her mother had become highly conflictual.

At the age of sixteen, F. had been interned in a psychiatric hospital for a catatonic episode that had followed her having *seen* "a sunset of sublime beauty." She had been treated on that occasion with psychotropic drugs, and had also been diagnosed as afflicted with BPD.

The symptoms that at present have led her to look for help are an unbearable sense of emptiness; anguished episodes of depersonalization and derealization; extreme anxiety; emotional instability with episodes of uncontainable rage; the inability to deal with abandon even on the part of persons of slight significance; accentuated sexual promiscuity. She is aware of using sex as a way of "holding on" to other people.

The overall photos of the sand constructions, as seen from the position in which the patient chose to work, are clear expressions of the workings of defense mechanisms such as splitting (Figures 1, 5), idealization (Figures 3, 4) and devaluation/idealization (Figures 2, 6).

Figure 7 on the other hand, signals the first appearance of contents connected with depression and sacrifice, even if isolated (the bag full of blood), and also of themes of substitutions for maternal care (the she-wolf, the kangaroo, the cradle, the bath-tub). In all the sand constructions, the analyst was seated at the upper left-hand corner of the sandbox.

Figure 1. Splitting

This is F.'s first sandbox. She has worked along the diagonal from the corner at the lower left to the one at the upper right. She has shaped two breasts in the sand. The upper left-hand corner holds a red, female devil and a dragon that grips a sphere (the world) in its claws. In the lower right-hand corner, a plaster figure of Aphrodite emerges from the sea. A number of figures have been placed around the breasts, as though in a circumambulation: to the left a dagger and a serpent; to the right a dolphin, an unsaddled horse, a jackal, a seal, and a butterfly. The breasts – prototypes, in Kleinian terms (1935, pp. 321-325; 1952, pp. 461-462 ff.) of 'good' and 'bad' partial objects – are separated (split from one another) by a pearl between two plaster capitals.

In the course of the session I felt quite weak, inert, and sleepy, as though empty and exhausted. This sense of torpor dissolved when I asked myself "To whom do those breasts belong? What kind of milk do they supply? Who's being fed, and who's doing the feeding? Is the suckling putting the mother to sleep as a way of facilitating nursing? Or is the goal to feed on *the good breast*, and to distance from *the bad breast*?"

That sense of discomfort (which often signals the presence of projective identification) took on more definite meaning when I read these extraordinary reflections on the part of Jung:

> Since empathy, like abstraction, is a conscious act, and since the latter is preceded by an unconscious projection, we may reasonably ask whether an unconscious act may not also precede empathy. As the essence of empathy is the projection of subjective contents, it follows that the preceding unconscious act must be its opposite – a neutralizing of the object that renders it inoperative. In this way the object is emptied, so to speak, robbed of its spontaneous activity, and thus made a suitable receptacle for subjective contents. [...] As a result of the unconscious act that precedes empathy, the sovereignty of the object is depotentiated, or rather it is overcompensated, because the subject immediately gains ascendancy over the object. This can only happen unconsciously, though an unconscious fantasy that either devalues and depotentiates the object or enhances the value and importance of the subject. (1921, pp. 292-3)

We're able here to appreciate the correlation between splitting, devaluation, idealization and projective identification.

Figure 2. Devaluation/Idealization

At the center of a clockwise vortex is a red dragon (the theme of the dragon is also present in sand constructions 1, 4 and 5) and standing in a circle around it are an unsaddled white horse that partly sinks into the sand (here again see Figures 1, 4 and 5) and three spherical marbles (two black, one red). At the outer edge of the vortex, to the left and right, a sea shell; above, an oval shield between two shells; below, four shells.

At the center of the sandbox we can make out a transverse line that virtually connects the two shells, the marbles, and the dragon. (A similar line is also found in Figure 7.)

In the upper left-hand corner of the sandbox: a saddled, bay horse and a shell. In the lower right-hand corner: a saddle, a dappled horse (see Figure 4) and a shell.

Figure 3. Idealization

51

The vortex develops clockwise, and has the shape of a question mark. At its center, a winged fairy. Along the path of the vortex: a black and white rabbit; a small white bear; and two brown bears, one of which plays with a butterfly (for the latter, see Figure 1); and three Native American girls (Pocahontas). Above and to the left, a winged tiger.

Figure 4. Idealization

A trench curves to the right, partly edged with colored marbles. Standing along it: a statue of the reunited sun and moon; a Venus figure (see Figures 1, 5); a pagan priestess with a shell; a dragon (already employed in the sandbox at Figure 1); a winged tiger (see Figure 3); a rearing, unsaddled, black horse, a fountain surmounted by a cupid; a geisha; Alice; Luna; Sol.

Figure 5. Splitting

F. traces out two vortices along the diagonal that runs from the upper left-hand corner to the lower right-hand corner. On the first vortex, an enchantress (Deianira), a servant girl and a geisha (already found in the sandbox at Figure 4), a pagan priestess (see Figure 4), the winged fairy (see Figure 3), an Aphrodite (see Figure 1), a squirrel, a koala, a sheet of blue crystal ('a fountain head') with two elephants and a dragon (see Figures 1 and 2) seated beside it.

Figure 6. Devaluation/ Idealization

At the center of a clockwise vortex in the form of a question mark (see Figure 2): a small angel; a miniature matrioska, in one piece; a shell; the whole surrounded by another twenty-five shells.

Lower, at center, at the bottom end of the question mark: a swan surrounded by nine shells, smaller than the ones before.

The upper left-hand corner, the lower left-hand corner, and the upper right-hand corner each contains a matrioska split in two. In the lower right-hand corner are two smaller matrioskas, likewise split in two.

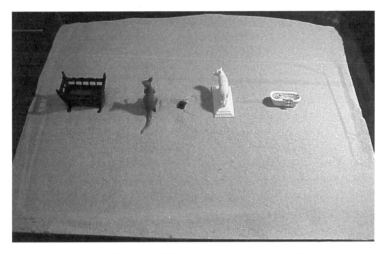

Figure 7. Themes of Depression and Maternal Care

A transverse line leads toward the center of the sandbox. (A similar line is found in Figure 5.) Along it, from left to right: a cradle; a female kangaroo with a baby kangaroo in her pouch; a sack filled with blood (see the dragon in Figure 5); the Capitoline she-wolf; a bath-tub filled with water, and also holding a small goose.

The she-wolf and the kangaroo are faced toward the analyst.

In the course of the treatment, the sandbox gradually became the place in which F. was able to represent, at one and the same time, maternal care and abandonment, acquisition and loss, meeting and separation. The acts the patient represented thus began to depart, even though gradually, from her habitual stereotypes. *Before*, she lacked a past of which the memory might be a consolation, and a future that might be desired or represent a hope; *now*, her time had ceased to lack all other dimensions than the present. Her feeling of desolation had thus begun to transform itself into nostalgia.

> The falling leaves drift by the window
> The autumn leaves of red and gold
> I see your lips, the summer kisses
> The sun-burned hands I used to hold
> Since you went away the days grow long
> And soon I'll hear old winter's song
> But I miss you most of all my darling
> When autumn leaves start to fall
>
> *C'est une chanson, qui nous ressemble*
> *Toi tu m'aimais et je t'aimais*
> *Nous vivions tous les deux ensemble*
> *Toi que m'aimais moi qui t'aimais*
> *Mais la vie sépare ceux qui s'aiment*
> *Tout doucement sans faire de bruit*
> *Et la mer efface sur le sable les pas des amants*
> *désunis.*

> Nat King Cole, *Autumn Leaves*
> (*Les Feuilles Mortes*)
> English lyrics by Johnny Mercer,
> French lyrics by Jacques Prévert

Vito La Spina

Note

I It's usual in discussions of BPD to recognize an ample recourse to projective identification, which is a defense that tends "to induce in the significant other what the subject *projects*, thus attempting to control the other." (Clarkin, Yeomans and Kernberg 1999, p. 7, my italics) But use of a visual metaphor is highly limiting. Quite to the contrary, "the concept of *resonance* [...] goes beyond the fragmentation of the Self and also recovers a sense of corporeal reality, since the metaphor of hearing, unlike that of seeing, in itself implies the presence of a *conscious, psychosomatic* level of perception." And more than anything else, "It directs attention to the whole of the analytic field, since it includes the experience of both of the members of the dyad.... It's by no means hard to imagine the nature and extent of the deepening of the therapeutic relationship if the analyst's responses to the patient's interventions (and vice versa) are understood as resonances which both have caused to vibrate. It's rather like the way a tuning fork is made to hum by another that rings at the same wave length." (Migliorati 2001, pp. 33-38)

References

Ammann, R. (1989): *Heilende Bilder der Seele: das Sandspiel der schöpferische Weg der Persönlichkeitsentwicklung,* München: Kösel-Verlag.

A.P.A. (1995): *DSM-IV Diagnostic and Statistical Manual of Mental Disorders,* Washington, DC: American Psychiatric Association.

Boyle, M. (1990): *Schizophrenia. A scientific delusion?,* London: Routledge.

Clarkin, J.F., Yeomans F.E., Kernberg O.F. (1999): *Psychotherapy for the Borderline Personality,* New York: John Wiley & Sons.

Colonna, M.T. (2000): "Grandi domande e risposte del nostro tempo," in "Sogni di una nuova era," *Rivista di Psicologia Analitica,* n. 9, 61.

Eliot, T.S. (1936-1942): "Four Quartets," *Collected Poems 1909–1962,* London: Faber and Faber.

Ellenberger, H.F. (1970): *The Discovery of the Unconscious. The History and Evolution of Dynamic Psychiatry,* New York: Basic Books.

Freud, S. (1911): *Formulierungen über die zwei Prinzipien des psychischen Geschehens,* GW VIII, sechste Auflage 1973, Frankfurt am Main: S. Fischer Verlag.

Gabbard, G.O. (1994): *Psychodynamic Psychiatry in Clinical Practice. The DSM-IV Edition,* Washington, DC: American Psychiatric Press.

Gabbard, G.O., Lester E.P. (1995): *Boundaries and Boundary Violations in Psychoanalysis*, New York: Basic Books.

Gabbard, G.O. (2001): "Empirical Evidence and Psychotherapy: A Growing Scientific Base," *Am J Psychiatry* 158:1, pp. 1-3.

Gessa, G.L., Serra, G. (1990): *Psicofarmacologia*, Milan: Masson.

Grunberger, B. (1989): *Narcisse et Anubis. Essais psychanalytique*, Paris: Éditions des femmes.

Gullotta, C. (2001): "*Evoluzione dell'orizzonte di coscienza attraverso l'esperienza del limite*," *Studi Junghiani* 14, pp. 7-20, Rome: FrancoAngeli.

Hoch, P., Polatin, P. (1949): "Pseudoneurotic forms of schizophrenia," *Psychiatric Quarterly*, 23, 248-276.

Jung, C.G. (1921): *Psychological Types*, CW vol. 6, Princeton: Princeton University Press.

Jung, C.G. (1935): *Analytical Psychology: Its Theory and Practice; The Tavistock Lectures*, CW vol. 18, Princeton: Princeton University Press.

Jung, C.G. (1946): *The Psychology of the Transference*, CW vol. 16, Princeton: Princeton University Press.

Jung, C.G. (1951): *Aion: Researches into the Phenomenology of the Self* CW, vol. 9, part II, Princeton: Princeton University Press.

Jung, C.G. (1947-1954): *On the Nature of the Psyche*, CW vol. 8, Princeton: Princeton University Press.

Jung, C.G. (1916-1958): *The Transcendent Function*, CW vol. 8, Princeton: Princeton University Press.

Jung, C.G. (1958): *Flying Saucers: A Modern Myth of Things Seen in the Skies*, CW vol. 10, Princeton: Princeton University Press.

Kalff, D.M. (1966): *Sandspiel*, Zurich: Rascher Verlag.

Kernberg, O.F. (1992): *Aggression in Personality Disorders and Perversions*, New Haven, CT: Yale University Press.

Klein, M. (1935): *A Contribution to the Psychogenesis of Manic-Depressive States*. In R. Money-Kyrle (Ed.) *The writings of Melanie Klein* (1984, Vol. 1, pp. 262-89), New York: The Free Press.

Klein, M. (1952): *Some Theoretical Conclusions Regarding the Emotional Life of the Infant*. In *Envy, Gratitude and Other Works, 1946-1963* (pp. 61-93), London: Hogarth Press.

Lichtenberg, J.D., Lachmann F.M., Fosshage J.L. (1992): *Self and Motivational Systems. Towards a theory of psychoanalytic technique*, Hillsdale, NJ: The Analytic Press.

Loriedo, C. (2002): "Prefazione," in: Loriedo C., Nardone G., Watzlawich P., Zeig J.K. (2002) *Strategie e stratagemmi della psicoterapia*, Rome: FrancoAngeli.

Mahler, M.S., Pine, F., Bergman, A. (1975): *The Psychological Birth of the Human Infant. Symbiosis and Individuation*, New York: Basic Books.

Maj, M. (1998) "Critique of the DSM–IV operational diagnostic criteria for schizophrenia," *British Journal of Psychiatry*, 172:458–460.

Migliorati, P. (2001): "Dal Faust al Doctor Faustus: una sfida impossibile?" *Studi Junghiani* 14, pp. 21-40, Rome: FrancoAngeli.

Montecchi, F. (1993): *Giocando con la sabbia. La psicoterapia con bambini e adolescenti e la "sand play therapy,"* Milan: FrancoAngeli.

Montecchi, F. (2000): Preface to the Italian edition (2000) of Ammann R. (1989) *Heilende Bilder der Seele: das Sandspiel der schöpferische Weg der Persönlichkeitsentwicklung.* Italian translation: *Sandplay: immagini che curano e trasformano. Una via creativa per lo sviluppo della personalità*, Milan: Vivarium.

Nivoli, G.C. (2001): *La patologia mentale del terapeuta e la patologia mentale del paziente: incontri e scontri*, Milan: Hippocrates.

Ovidio (3-8): *Metamorphoses*, translated by Sir Samuel Garth, John Dryden, et al.

Panepucci, A. (2000): "Vivere senza simboli," in "Sogni di una nuova era," *Rivista di Psicologia Analitica*, n. 9, 61.

Rossi, Monti M., Stanghellini G. (Eds.) (1999): *Psicopatologia della schizofrenia. Prospettive metodologiche e cliniche*, Milan: Cortina.

Searles, H.F. (1976): *Transitional Phenomena and Therapeutic Symbiosis.* In Searles H.F. (1979) *Countertransference and Related Subjects*, Madison, CT: International Universities Press.

Sedgwick, D. (1995): *The Wounded Healer: Countertransference from a Jungian Perspective*, London: Routledge.

von Franz, M.L. (1971): *The Inferior Function.* In Hillman J. (1979) *Lectures on Jung's typology*, Irving, Texas: Spring Publications.

von Franz, M.L. (1988): *Psyche und Materie*, Einsiedeln: Daimon Verlag.

Winnicott, D.W. (1965): *The Maturational Process and the Facilitating Environment. Studies in the Theory of Emotional Development*, New York: International Universities Press.

W.H.O. (1992): *The ICD-10. Classification of Mental and Behavioural Disorders: clinical descriptions and diagnostic guidelines*, Geneve: World Health Organization.

Zoja, L. (1999): *Coltivare l'anima*, Bergamo: Moretti & Vitali, 2001.

Matter and the Psyche: A Feasible Therapy

Andreina Navone

I started working with sandplay thirty-two years ago. My training began with Dora Kalff; my experience with sandplay then grew richer and further developed as it turned in the course of time into an integrated part of my analytical training, and as well of my practice as a therapist.

Over the last few years, I have lent particular attention to the problems concerning the primary relationship and the first years of development, to the connection between such problems and the moment at which sandplay entered therapy, and to the way the patients touched, handled and held the sand, allowing it to slip through their fingers. I have been especially interested in sandplay constructions that make no use of objects or miniatures, and where sand itself, either wet or dry, takes on the connotation of a kind of primordial matter.

We know that the nature of an individual – the way an individual "is," and how he or she relates to the world – is deeply marked by the first stages of his or her existence. We know that while proceeding though the whole of a life an individual will always bear a unique and peculiar imprint which is highly charged with meaning, and which constantly alters the individual and the life the individual leads. It is precisely this experience, of the imprint that marks a human being, that all our patients – whatever their age, ethnic group, symptoms or pathology – present to us through their suffering.

But even before I began to reflect on sandplay images that make no use of objects or miniatures, my thoughts on these subjects had found a point of departure in the observation of a profoundly meaningful drawing made by an adopted child during his final session of therapy. It was the image of a brown egg, an earthen color (created by mixing many colors) or, if you prefer, the color of cinnamon (an important element that emerged during therapy). It showed how the therapeutic relationship, in regression, had activated contact at a very deep level. It gave the feeling of coming face to face with a representation of raw matter, as the first and most basic reference point for an experience of taking root on terms which had grown both tangible and reassuring. For the therapist, it also entailed a perception of the synergy of body and psyche, of the absolute uniqueness of the individual human being who takes on a body that's made of matter but who also is able – through containment and recognition – to open up to psychic life through the flow of continuous creation.

During the final period of our work, the patient (twelve years old) would usually bring sticks of cinnamon to our sessions. He wanted us to taste them together, even while also suggesting that the cinnamon might be poisonous.

Analyst: Do you think the herbalist would sell it if it were poisonous?

Child: No, I really don't think so.

Analyst: Then we can find out what it tastes like.

Child: Cinnamon burns like pepper but … learning something new requires a sacrifice.

Analyst: Maybe that's why it's important not to be alone, so you can talk about what happens.

Child: I have to find out where cinnamon comes from.

After this session the boy began to give signs of wanting to bring therapy to a close. During the following session, he first put a child (a doll) in a large box together with a monkey he had saved from abandonment and raised in the therapy studio. It was then, for the very first time, that he asked to paint, with the use of brushes and colors.

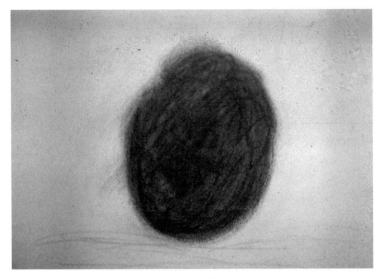

Figure 1

So on a white sheet of paper a cinnamon-colored egg slowly took shape – first suspended in emptiness, then later resting on a sketchy line of earth. The egg's emergence in the space of acceptance and protection represented the boy's discovery of his unconscious roots, and his contact and confrontation with them. This vital discovery was no less precious than his life itself, and, as such, it had to be protected and kept indelible in a safe container. After completing his drawing the boy had said, "This should be kept in a museum."

The sharing of risk, fear, and courage, and the discovery of the taste of cinnamon – which is peppery rather than sweet, as the uninitiated might not imagine – were a part of the experience of a possible union. The museum that hosts the drawing is to provide a space in which it can be witnessed, and the act takes on meaning by virtue of its transformation into an experience of belonging.

The representation of a primary object was thus to be preserved in an egg and in a museum; and it will continue to be present for the patient after he has parted with it, since now it is part of the Self, like a loom on which it is finally possible to begin the weaving of relational dynamics in ways which never before had been foreseen.

Emanuele was no longer a rootless fragment of a child. He at last had reached a recognition of his own value, of his own uniqueness, and he had made that discovery not only in the symbolic space of the therapy setting, but also in that other space where his biological parents – although both of us were unacquainted with them – had always met with his acceptance and recognition.

The process entailed in regression had been able to reach those positive archetypal forms and energies on which the species nourishes itself at undifferentiated levels, and which the individual can contact and integrate only if protected and contained within a project that finds its exclusive focus in him/herself.

It has now grown clear to me that some patients feel the need to abandon themselves, entrusting themselves to a wordless experience expressed through sand. They communicate this experience only through movements and imprints, as though returning to a past in which to discover and attempt to recreate the very first forms of sensorial, somatic, kinetic writing, devoid of any specific dimension of signification. They shape and represent this writing in raw matter, bringing it to the same corporeal level as gesticulation, which is also to say that these feelings and kinetic impressions – these wordless signs which can only be understood empathetically – are accepted in the very same moment in which they emerge. These patients have found it possible to begin to offer space and recognition to the non-spoken, to the shapeless, to that other side of things which has remained encapsulated, and repressed, and deprived of all nourishment. They have begun to imagine the possibility of being able to touch and to think it, of being able to read its ancient, vital tales. This can signal the beginning of an experience which analyst and patient are able to share, an opening out towards a dynamic of integration, a first experience of the Self and the world, an experience of the original Self.

We know that everything that happens in the therapeutic setting has a meaning. So, when a patient touches, handles and manipulates the sand we have to accept that perhaps we do not understand. We might speak of a state of tension, or even of torment, but we stand within an experience that demands lucidity, patience and constancy; we stand before a form of defense that turns a small and seemingly unintelligible event into a matter of great importance, into something to be stored and safeguarded in a free and protected space so that it will not once again fall back into the limbo of unconsciousness.

It is fundamental to acknowledge all this, but even more important to recognize that this is not enough. Awareness and empathy must be seen as the premise for a much more complex therapeutic experience, which is the experience of working with our countertransference in ways that structure and give access to the analytic methodology which is the fundamental tool of Jungian therapy.

The sandbox thus becomes a setting inside the therapeutic setting, and what comes to expression by way of it has the features of something more than insightful spontaneity: what in fact it expresses is a fully analytical experience and a feasible reflection on such an experience.

I agree with Searles when she writes "... in the analytic process of maturation or recovery it is not possible to be freed from what is felt; on the contrary, one becomes ever freer to experience all kinds of emotions and feelings." (Searles, 22 TR.IT. 1994. *The Countertransference*. Turin: Boringhieri)

So, the attention paid to the unconscious must be directed not only to the patient's unconscious but also to the therapist's. We know that listening, tension, and attention activate the emotions in the area of the analytical relationship, where the rigorous calibration of a space and a presence can make it constantly possible to offer containment and acceptance as well as elaboration and restitution.

As well, one has to remember that regression is a temporary condition, but that it nonetheless returns to the setting again and again, determining the quality of what one hears, and also of what one sees. It is necessary too to reflect on distance and identification, remembering that the latter is a way of knowing that can be accompanied by the risk of fusion, whereas the therapist's subjectivity has to be safeguarded.

I remember that during certain sessions I felt trapped in a timeless silence, empty even of the sound of silence, as if facing a sort of raw matter. It was a phenomenon connected with the beginnings of things, and with the absence of points of reference. It was the feeling of being in the presence of something new which never before had been investigated, and which also might grow frustrated and make its escape if its process of becoming and manifestation were not defended.

The following sequence of sandbox images comes from the case of young woman, at thirty-eight years of age.

One day the voice of a woman totally unknown to me left the following message on my answering machine: "264789." She added nothing more, and her tone was hurried and almost annoyed.

A little surprised, I thought, "Is this possible?" And I answered, "Obviously it is."

Somewhat overreacting, I decided that I did not want to deal with a telephone number that had burst with that tone into my office. But I also knew it would call up images which I surely couldn't avoid.

I should say that at the time my answering machine asked callers to leave a number if they wanted me to call them back. The woman in question seemed to have synthesized the whole of herself into a number, or to have introduced herself as though she were only a number. This brought back cruel and unforgettable memories and a deathly sensation of devaluation or, even worse, of depersonalization and self-rejection; this was why I decided not to allow myself to be infected by any such arrogance. So, I waited.

After a while came a second request, formulated in the same manner. It was clear that Ms. "phone number" wanted an appointment and expected me to call her back.

With the second phone call, the impact of the caller's arrogance was much less forceful. It gave rise, in fact, to an image: the hand of a child who was secretly throwing a stone and immediately hiding her hand, in expectation of an immediate reaction.

I told myself that this would not be easy. But the only way to assess this request to play a game was by acting the way I would with a child, which is to say by playing the game:

"Who could possibly have thrown that stone? I guess I'll go and look for her ..."

"Where could she be? She's not here, or over there ..."

So the child abandons her hiding place and, full of joy, amazement and innocence, cries out:

"It's me! I'm here."

And so:

"Now I've caught you ..."

And only then is there a glimpse of some first movement; only then does one really get underway, and the game begins!

In fact, the phone number was shortly later preceded by a name and a request for an appointment, still in a highly impersonal, indifferent tone. But the game had now begun, and had a space in which to happen, and a partner prepared to play it.

As I write, I remember Dora Kalff's assessment of children's hiding – for example, when they ring the doorbell and then quickly hide out of sight, or when they want to play hide-and-seek. Sometimes they make certain characters play such games; or children hide such figures, even in the sandbox of the therapy room, along with other objects that likewise disappear from view, while still remaining there. To find them, one must sometimes play a guessing game, or go on a hunt to search them out. Dora Kalff considered such hiding games to be a gesture of the Self, a symptom that spurs the other to pay attention to me, to look for me, to find me, to discover all the hidden things which are not the way they ought to be and which cannot be expressed, to look for all the good things which I am hiding from myself and which, if found, could once again give me peace and safety. Dora Kalff always saw the symptom as a first undertaking on the part of the Self, as a potential directed toward the integration of opposites, and the healing of splits.

This young woman suffered from a serious relational problem. As far as she could see, all objects were necessarily disposable – including her analyst. This seemed to give her the possibility of exercising rigorous control over a life made up only of work, and of sex which was totally devoid of feeling.

With her, as in other similar cases (narcissistic pathologies, identity crises, adoptions), the first session of therapy used only words for describing, for narrating, for criticizing – words that seemed to occupy the whole space of the session, and all the emotions and images of the patent's split.

Sandplay, in such a context, is ridiculed: it's seen as a children's amusement, and as something silly if employed by grown-ups.

For some time I found myself dealing with behavior that oscillated between exasperating provocations, and attitudes of seduction. For example, it sometimes happened that I'd open the door and find myself looking at a newspaper that hid nearly half the person standing behind it (the patient was not tall); and she would fold it only after finishing reading what interested her. Or, I'd open the door and might find myself faced by an enormous, ostentatious, yellow ice cream cone which she continued to lick with indifference until it was finished.

Once she had sat down in her chair, she would nearly always take off her shoes, accompanying the action with a childish, apologetic smile, as though saying "sorry," but she nonetheless did as she pleased, without hesitation.

Her provocations disturbed me and felt like physical blows, and at times seemed unbearable. Yet those were precisely the moments when the image of that hiding child – perhaps in tears – would appear: a child who had started an aggressive game so as then to be able to say that no one, really, had ever taken care of her, as though she had never been seen and therefore, as well, never looked for. It was the image of a child who had been left on her own too soon, who had grown up quickly after early abandonment, but who still, desperately and in spite of everything, was waiting.

One day she recounted a dream, hurled at me nearly as a challenge, that marked a turning point in my experience of her situation.

The patient had found herself walking down a street flanked by transparent houses with no walls. In some houses, uninteresting family scenes took place. Strange beings – perhaps from other worlds – were moving about in others, but again she remained entirely indifferent to them. But she wanted out of simple curiosity to continue her walk: she wanted to see what lay at the end of it. Continuing to walk, she reached a sort of central square where she expected to find something special. Instead, there was nothing at all. She turned back a little disappointed, but with nearly complete indifference.

It was a dream that left a feeling of flat desolation, but which ultimately mirrored the atmosphere of the life she was leading: a life in a dimension where everything was strained; a life without emotion, where she was often compelled to attack as a way of defending herself, never relaxed, with always swollen feet and a nervous stomach. Only her curiosity had been rescued from so much desolation.

The dream gave me a physical sensation of absence and uneasiness, and as well I felt immersed in an atmosphere in which absolute silence was accompanied by the deathly immobility of a cold, airless limbo. The only vibration I perceived was the patient's curiosity, which in spite of everything had carried her along in its wake, and seemed to continue to be her driving force.

I accepted and welcomed that vibration as though it were a gift. And that atmosphere gave issue to an image that very much moved me at the time. It was an image of E.T. – the small, lost and desperate extra-terrestrial in Spielberg's film – and, more precisely, from the sequence in which a boy drops his ball. Someone, in spite of fear and shock, throws it back, instinctively entrusting himself to the only universal language: the playing of games.

In much the same way, the patient's curiosity seemed to bounce back and forth between us. This apparently imperceptible vibration in the petrified atmosphere of the dream was a tiny space of mutual comprehension. But more than anything else it contained that hopeless desperation which instinctively had dragged her into the only known universal language: play. And so, with a certain amount of hesitation, she asked if she could work with the sandbox.

The expression on her face – which was often sardonic and unfriendly even when she smiled – had slowly become relaxed, allowing a glimpse of the features of an undefended, shy and thoughtful little girl. I can still see clearly how she held the sand in her hands, her wary attitude:

"But what am I doing? What does this mean?" she whispered. Meanwhile, one had the impression of witnessing an immersion into some ancient, primordial form of matter that had to be explored with care. More than a movement linked to regression, one perceived an intense and powerful emotion that derived from contact with a kind of undifferentiated "primal magma," and from the possibility of allowing it expression in a shared and protected space.

It was like suddenly finding oneself re-immersed in a primary charge of emotion, like those experienced in the first phase of life as the body attempts to relate to, and to assimilate, what dawns with every new experience; but the body is not yet capable of elaborating these corporeal signals which will later be able to mark other images as having the qualities of good or bad, or as sources of pleasure or pain.

Observing some of these creations, we see that the sand has been mixed, poured from one hand to the other, patted down, but then immediately stirred again. (Figure 2) Some show rudimentary attempts to make more recognizable shapes, such as the sun and the moon (Figure 3), outlines of caverns or walls (Figure 4). This attempt to create form, attempting to give it a context, only then to destroy it and start all over again, went on for some time. Then finally one day something different suddenly coalesced. It was the sketch of a figure in which it was possible to recognize a little girl in a horizontal position (Figure 5). It communicated a feeling of intense cold, perhaps because the sand was quite wet. That great coldness became the source of a very clear image: the pattern of an ice crystal. An eternal, primordial shape, always ready to materialize when temperatures sufficiently drop, but invisible and elusive until a snowflake appears.

Figure 2

Figure 3

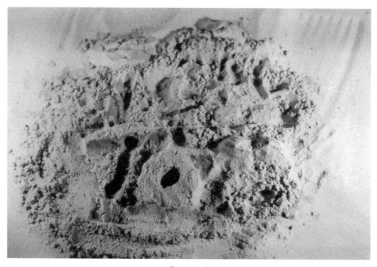

Figure 4

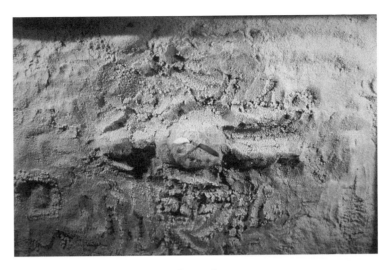

Figure 5

The little girl lay horizontally on dark earth. Was she waiting perhaps for the right temperature before transforming into a child of warm flesh and blood?

But she would never have been just any little girl, since a special place was needed in which to regulate heat (not too much), desire (not only mine), fear (not to be projected). These things, right here and now, were for her alone: emotion, heat, tension, attention, elaboration, restitution, all gathered together and made available within the therapeutic space, enlivening the possibility of reconstructing a new gestation: an "as if" gestation which in any case will be sufficient to show the analyst that she has rediscovered and entered into contact with a part of herself that's able to become involved in a project for a new birth.

Sometimes, as soon as I came closer the little girl would retreat, close up, pretend to be lifeless. But even so, while waiting, almost in a state of suspension, there was an image now fixed in my mind. Contact had been established: a representation. She had thrown her last stone, but she had not hidden, and she could no longer conceal her hand since it seemed that I could feel it, frail and tiny, within my own, and I could hold it. There was no longer any question as to who would take the first step; at this point, it was possible to run a risk, and to wait.

The latest disappointment she had suffered in her daily life had left her prostrated. Believing for the umpteenth time that she had controlled a situation that regularly repeated the cliched pattern of "throw-away-after-use," she instead had felt herself to have been used and discarded. Suddenly assailed by the perception of "a different kind of pain" (her words), she asked herself why there was nothing more to say when sex was over and done with. The only remaining desire was to slip away into a desperate silence where feelings, sensations, words and memories had no way to find a space into which to inscribe a memory or reflection on the experiences she had lived through.

Figure 6

This was the first occasion on which she allowed herself to face her anguish and fragility on a more profound level, and to speak of her fear and shame. She was aching and bewildered, but had greater freedom to suffer and fight, and as well to liberate into this suffering the possibility of a new experience of life – the experience of the vital energies, both positive and negative, that we have to face every day, starting not only at birth, but from the moment of our conception.

This is the way she depicted this turning point. (Figure 6)

A mountain. Distinctly carved into its sides are steps recalling those of Mayan constructions. At its peak, two shapeless but erect elements stand one before the other, linked by a kind of bridge. At the same time, coming up from a gully sketched on one side of the mountain, a third erect element seems to be on its way to the summit. (Figure 7 and Figure 8)

It is obvious when a mode of working passes from an always two-dimensional and exclusively horizontal plane to a three-dimensional system of co-ordinates which are also inclusive of verticality. Undertakings may still be shapeless, but their placement is precise, and they discover rudimentary expression. The striking thing is the dynamic which, in spite of everything else, these figures manage to express: an energy that moves towards the representation of the archetypal form of union. They have been transformed by their passage from two to three, through the agency of a material such as sand, in which the fundamental experience of matter, and the body, and the energy that unites them has taken place.

But above all we find ourselves faced with a symbolic reconstruction of the elements at the base of every creation. My reference is less to mother, father and child – or to any primary relationship that comes to exist at a subsequent time – than to the magic moment that sets in motion the birth of life.

Figure 7

Figure 8

This setting of life in motion – here represented in terms of its essential elements – will later be able to reconstruct itself in the area of the affects, which – according to Jung – are the organizing principles of psychic life. In this case, however, it inevitably leads us as well to an encounter with the core of a complicated, affective atonality in its most archaic form, which is to say at the level of the proto-affects, which in previous sandplay images had remained undifferentiated.

The shapes just barely outlined in the sand seem to hold the possibility of energizing a dialectic process for the differentiation of the emotions. With the help of language, this process in turn will slowly grow able to transform itself, and then to express itself through feelings which have the power to communicate with the interior state of the patient's Self, thus allowing her entrance into a life of relationships with others. In other words, she will exit the area of archaic complexes in order to enter the area of her personal complexes.

In relating this experience today, I can see more clearly how all the preceding verbal work had taken place on two levels. The first of these levels can be described as a narrative discourse through which the patient could express her provocations and acts of aggression, and find them accepted and contained by the therapeutic space. Here at this level, emotional responses were mostly concerned with her body, the feelings of which had always remained in the background – relegated only to sexual functions or somatizations – whereas her mind was always very active.

The other level can be described as the patient's attempt to manage her ambivalent relationship with analysis, and with the analyst as an incarnation of a bridge-like function. The patient shifted constantly back and forth between a defensive attitude, and the desire – but mixed with fear – to break through barriers and to enter the deep, non-verbal spaces in which her ancient, petrified pain had found its secret refuge.

At a certain point, we both had to make a choice. On the one hand, the process allowed the emergence of the level of the primary process experienced in the initial stage of life. But, on the other, the analytical experience simultaneously and inevitably thrust us towards the secondary processes linked to reflection, reasoning, decision-making, emotions and feelings.

It was very difficult for this patient to allow her infantile emotions to take on a mental representation, owing to the very clear fact that nearly no psychic meaning had been attributed to particular childhood experiences (Sidoli 1993, p.175).

The violence of the rejection experienced by the patient had produced dissociative defenses that did not allow – in fact, had annulled – the integrative experience of the archetype: links between affect and image had been severed, thus rendering the experience of rejection meaningless.

In cases such as these, no memory of the experience is retained, since as soon as the possibility of an integration arises, the ego is threatened by the potential repetition of an intolerable experience, or by a new unbearable emotion, and the experience is therefore split off.

But sandplay gave these few meager elements the possibility of entering a healing process that reconnected the body and the mind. The experience of acceptance had loosened rigidities and mitigated fears, and little by little had freed that sense of Self which is able to elaborate the emotional signals that come from the body and the images that derive from them.

When put into contact with others, such images allow us to confer different qualities to our emotions, and as well to new images, reestablishing contact with the experiences of perception and evaluation to which I refer as "primary evaluations," which consist of a dynamic of opposites such as pleasure-pain, hot-cold, in-out, acceptance-refusal, and this is very much a bodily experience. The body allows us to structure the feeling of what makes us conscious of something in the process of defining itself, in the process of taking shape. And as tension gradually relaxes, figures of shapeless matter or material can appear in the sand, as in fact occurred in this case – figures which the mind is perhaps unable to decipher, but which the feelings can accept, reunite and transform through metaphor. This is what Dora Kalff meant when she spoke of having an "experience" while working with sand.

Referring again to primary evaluations, we know that the child's unaccepted and non-elaborated anxieties remain nameless, archaic terrors that undermine the construction of identity, thus opening the way for a pathology to be structured. But before appearing in behavior, the deviation is nurtured in fantasy. In other words, in the course of time it comes to be rooted in ways that exert a negative influence on the experience and evaluation of reality. Every relational experience is always lived out on the terms of such unconscious fantasies, which operate at the deepest emotional levels. They involve, on the one hand, an imagined action, and, on the other, the emotional dynamics which the child activates as a defense: dynamics such as retreat, escape, magical expectations, aversion, envy, fear, aggressiveness and the desire for the exclusive possession of objects.

Unconscious fantasy is not a synonym for imagination. Imagination is something that one experiences by way of the image-filled constructions through which it represents itself, whereas unconscious fantasy is the functional base that precedes all capacity for representation. Unconscious fantasy can emotionally color reality (beautiful-ugly, good-bad, pleasant-unpleasant). It is on the same level as the primary processes; it is pure energy; it is created before verbal expression; it is rooted in corporeal experience (somatization, neonatal rage, etc.); and it is colored with omnipotence and extremism. Unconscious fantasy is also responsible for the psychic classification of needs – satisfied needs make the object good, unsatisfied needs make the object bad; the dynamics involved are those of pleasure and pain, and the principle invoked is "all or nothing." On the basis of fantasy experience, reality is evaluated as good or bad. And it's on this basis that the child establishes behavior that seeks closeness (love) and distance (hate): these behavior patterns result from evaluations which are instant, emotional, and primordial, and not rational and realistic, but psychic and impulsive.

These very first attitudes determine whether one will be more open or closed in relationships with people and things; whether one will have more or less interest in the exterior world, and thus a foundation for greater or lesser adaptability; they determine one's levels of interest, curiosity, participation. They likewise determine the constellation of an optimistic, receptive, intelligent attitude towards life, as opposed to the opposite: closure, apathy, flagging attention, mental impoverishment.

So, unconscious fantasy – or, in other words, the basic way in which one evaluates reality – has to be understood as the initial mode for the elaboration of energies, rather on the order of a first filter that regulates the passage of the disruptive energies of impulse into the realm of action.

Every psychic act is marked by circular relationships between information, emotion, and action: such circularity is one of life's fundamental elements, and lies at the origins of its dynamics of development.

This sandbox image was a determining factor in the progress of the therapeutic process, and I would like to underscore how great a force of transformation was represented in a few barely outlined shapes that gave expression to the projects and energies which had come to be released by a therapeutic relationship of transference and countertransference.

The images that followed were highly significant: an imprint of the two hands – bodily organs on the search for suitable shapes – (Figure 9) and a kind of rudimentary castle, a *temenos* that's able to contain, defend, welcome … (Figure 10).

There is the vaguely-outlined couple on the mountain top: one sees two different shapes, which are possibly male and female forms, united by a bridge. They show us the possibilities enclosed in a fecund encounter with a third person: with the new, and all its energy for propelling us along the path of the evolution of both the individual and the species; with the act of conception that springs from the union of opposites. It's here that the individual is able to experience and activate the archetypal triad; and it's here that one sees the emergence of a possibility of "relationship." This is what grew clear as the case developed further.

Figure 9

Figure 10

The patient too accepted the little girl drawn in the sand as a force of integration and resolution within her cognitive process, in which the integration of opposites and otherness allowed her to experience the unavoidable paradox of dependence and autonomy as elements which ceased to be divided, and which function in dynamic synergy in the daily experience of life.

So, sandplay imagery in which there are no objects presents us with situations that don't involve regressing with the patient, as happens in corrective analysis. One will be faced instead with the emergence of something that was already potential in the patient. Such imagery is indicative of an environment of phenomena which don't discover their representation on the basis of a point of departure from a relatively mature and adult condition; they begin, instead, to emerge since they have never done so before. This too, yes, comes about by way of regression; but I'd run the risk of calling it a regression that takes the form of a re-immersion in matter itself (which is here a re-immersion in sand). Such phenomena seem to come about in an environment of thoughts that have never been thought before, and of affects which have never before been represented: it's a place where the discovery of forms and objects is also the act of creating them. So, a protected space is contained in the ability to give adequate response to all the stages of the patient's life that the transference re-proposes – including conception, pregnancy and birth – but which the analyst holds in custody, supports, and gives back in an act of restitution.

The image of an emptiness leads up through a series of abandonments (wishes, expectations, projects, interpretations) to the way things stand, while waiting for the matter at the base of things to emerge from therapy itself, and as well for both patient and analyst to sink their roots into a state of undefined potential, which for both of them constitutes a stimulus and a therapeutic activity.

Children in Distress

Stefano Marinucci

This discussion of violence encountered by children won't lend particular attention to the kinds of abuse which are typically found in the world's poorer countries, or in those in a chronic state of war. In such situations the primary drive for pure and simple survival promotes scant respect for anyone's rights, no matter if an adult or a child, since their only controlling rule is the primitive law of the stronger. The means through which to change such situations will only be found in a series of radical, world-wide transformations, first of all at the economic level, and they therefore lie beyond the scope of these comments. In the context of our western culture, I will also proceed without unduly emphasizing the forms of physical or sexual abuse that so clamorously but intermittently explode into the view of the mass media. While doubtless especially grave, these forms of abuse are finally nothing more than the most sordid manifestations of a much more vast and complex phenomenon; and just as they suddenly burst into the media, they're newly forgotten with equal speed, distracting attention from the true problem, which is the daily psychological violence to which children are often exposed. Such violence supplies the terrain in which more extreme phenomena grow, and in turn it finds its cultural roots in the typically violent ways, often cunningly concealed, in which our society articulates social relationships.

The psychological violence inflicted on children is in fact more insidious than physical and sexual abuse, and it is often difficult to discover and treat since its borders are indistinct, growing confused on the one hand with rigid pedagogical attitudes, on the other with patterns of behavior which typify neglect. While seeming to be less dramatic, it holds deeper consequences for the structure of the child's psyche; it is also more destructive in terms of the developmental processes that minors normally experience. Psychological violence is marked in fact by a number of specific features that account for its high pathogenic potential (Marinucci 1998):

1) It first begins to be exercised in a very precocious period in the life of the child, even at times predating birth; it's inflicted in any event on very young and extremely vulnerable subjects.

2) It is exercised for a very long period of time before its destructive consequences grow manifest in the individual.

3) It is almost never exercised directly, and develops instead through the deployment of ambiguous and paradoxical messages from which the child has no possibility of self-defense.

This last aspect of psychological violence constitutes its most harmful feature. Whereas children who have fallen victim to a clear and definite form of physical or sexual abuse may still be capable, even if in oppositional terms, of structuring autonomous, functional personalities, this isn't the case for children who find themselves confronted with something that shows no definite characteristics. When violence is subtle, ambiguous, and couched in terms that the child finds totally incomprehensible, the result can be a profound distortion of the child's whole process of growth, and the child will encounter insurmountable difficulties in the structuring of a viable Self, even in a defensive key. This, in fact, is the form of violence that lies at the roots of the most serious forms of psychopathology, and they often don't come to light until the moment of a sudden and dramatic collapse of the psychic structure of the child who has been immersed in it.

For a clearer understanding of the way in which children fall victim to these kinds of distress, we must briefly review the background situation, and how it develops in the course of time.

Well before birth, a child already occupies a space in its parents' minds. This is a space within their fantasies, and its nature derives from a number of different factors:

1) the personality characteristics of the individual parents;
2) the quality of the parents' relationship as a couple;
3) the way the couple relates to its social environment.

This is to say that the mental space in which the child exists is created by its parents on the basis of their individual personalities, of the original motivations that led them to form a couple, of the further evolution of their relation as a couple, and, finally, of how they relate to their larger social environment, which is to speak of the families from which they come, of the work they do, of their relations with friends, and of the whole gamut of difficulties and expectations that these various realities activate within them. It's a question, finally, of a kind of "psychological cradle" that consists primarily of personal and family projections, of projects and hopes, but also of fears and anxieties, and parents deposit their fantasy child in such a cradle months before their real child enters the world. It's enough to remember the sometimes obstinate desire to have a child, or, on the other hand, the unwanted child; or the complex set of fantasies that lie behind the hope that a child be male or female; or again the possible conflicts between motherhood and a mother's career possibilities. These are only a few examples of fantasies and emotional contents that have nothing to do with the real child, but which at birth weigh down on its shoulders and condition its future relationship with the circumambient world.

During the period of expecting a child, it is physiologically inevitable for fantasies to be activated in its parents and in the surrounding social environment; indeed, it would be highly pathological for such a thing not to happen. Apart from the question of certain contents, what characterizes fantasies which are dangerous for the child lies in their quality. The rigidity of pedagogical or ideological positions, the capacity of a number of mental constructions to alter the function of the parents, insensitivity or indifference to real conditions which may prove to differ from those which were fantasized are elements that predispose parents and the environment to construct a reality that can damage a child's development.

What's needed, indeed, for harmonious development is that the mental space prepared for the child be sufficiently free of fantasies with pathological content, and that it function as an elastic container that can adapt to the personal characteristics of the child who is about to be born, and who will have to occupy it.

The child, after all, is by no means a *tabula rasa*, and, quite the contrary, possesses an individual personality, even if largely at the level of potential. The child already possesses what Jung called "the Self," which is a genetically programmed structure that gradually unfolds into a well articulated archetype, as organized by its affective relation with the environment. The central kernel of the child's personality is already active long before birth, as can easily be deduced, for example, from the stories mothers tell about their experiences of emotional exchange with the child from the time of the start of intrauterine fetal movements. Remembering the various sensations transmitted by more and less active fetuses, some mothers speak of a child who "has always been active and energetic, starting from the time inside my belly." Others speak of children who from early on were a source of concern since they "moved too little." Such emotional exchanges are mediated by neurotransmitters that cross the placental barrier in both directions, so that mother and child reciprocally influence their shared psychophysical circuit. So, the newborn child doesn't passively experience a unidirectional, adult-to-child relationship which is progressively modeled as the adult desires; the child establishes a bi-directional relationship in which the behavior of each of two partners influences and modifies the behavior of the other.

So, in addition to the growth of a child that's nested in its mother's womb, the course of a pregnancy also sees the creation of a psychic child in its mother's mind, and this imaginary child is also the fruit of the fantasies of all the members of the extended family. By way of the affective and corporeal exchanges that set up relations of empathetic communication between mother and fetus, every mother in the course of gestation learns to known her child, and in doing so also lays the basis for exchange and communication in the period after birth. The ease of such communication will depend on the degree to which she's able to unite the psychic child with the real child, and as well on the extent of her comfort with her own physical transformation and with her physical perception of the fetus; the movements of the fetus, the sound of its heartbeat, and the whole range of modern scientific instruments that offer the mother a rational perception of the unborn child (ultrasound imagery, laboratory analyses, amniocentesis, childbirth training, and so forth) all contribute to bringing about the so-called "pregnancy regression." The mother's involvement in the construction of a mental space for the child she's about to bear is the reason for which it is indispensable in the course of a pregnancy to offer support to the mother-to-be, and likewise to awaken and promote the support that can come from the father and as well from other environmental resources in the period of gestation and then in the first months of the life of the newborn child. So, there's a very great flaw in the stereotype that sees the birth and rearing of disturbed children as entirely and personally their mother's responsibility.

In order to offer a mental space to another person, one must first of all be capable of listening to oneself: to one's own past, one's own present-day experience, one's own desires and needs for the future. Any nexus of unconscious problems that remains ignored or non-elaborated profoundly alters a person's sensitivity to the other, and thus the ability to live with the other, since others become objects of unconscious projections that alter their personal characteristics finally to the point of disallowing their maintenance of an autonomous existence.

All the forms of psychic distress that occur in the period of childhood derive from this one root: from an altered or insufficient perception on the part of the parent of the real needs of that single, individual child, and from the difficulties that the child encounters as a consequence, and finds insurmountable. In short, the parent's mind, from the very start, doesn't offer the child the kind of container that allows for development and evolution.

The ability to understand a child, and to see that the child's demands are different from those of the adults in his or her environment implies the parents' capacity to regress to an awareness of an infant's fundamental needs, and to establish specific contact with that one, particular, growing personality. But this process is empathetic, and can therefore be disturbed by any number of factors in the parent's interior world, no less than by the quality and timeliness of the cares and attentions which the parent provides.

The condition of the newborn child is a condition of extreme vulnerability. The child, in fact, is born with highly rudimentary means of defense and is destined to die if it is not nourished, protected and cared for by an adult who's capable of providing for all its essential needs, with all attendant, necessary regularity. But beyond all questions of the adequacy of physical care, the central issue for the child's psychological development – as students of psychological evolution have been able to show for quite some time – lies in the emotional quality of the care the parents provide, which is also to speak of the intentions that guide the performance of their daily tasks. Succinctly put, the relational meaning of the care provided is the factor that counts as fundamental. The child, in fact, has the need to feel loved for the simple fact of existing. As well there's the need to be able to count on a parental figure who helps them overcome the anguish that derives from an initial state of total impotence, who respects their fears and insecurities, who deciphers reality for them, who helps them to fulfill their desires, allowing them to test their limits but without compromising their fundamental sense of self-confidence.

The specific causes of psychic distress among children are of course quite numerous and vary from case to case, depending on the parents as individuals, as well as on specific facts and levels of social communication and collective imagination. But we can group them schematically into the following categories:

a) the presence in the parents of a major psychopathology, such as psychosis, personality disorders, etc.,

b) situations of socio-economic hardship, flanked by demands that the child be a vehicle of social promotion,

c) parental dependence on distorted messages from the mass media, with habitual, non-critical reception of stereotypes,

d) the persistence of mythical visions of childhood in the collective imagination,

e) situations where the child is a witness to episodes of family violence,

f) a group of "new" causes that derive from situations of social change that offer no more than apparent redress for older forms of violence.

I have discussed these causes in detail in another text (Marinucci 2003). Here I'll consider only two of them, the second and the last, with accompanying examples of the cases of children who were treated with sandplay therapy.

Situations of Socio-Economic Hardship

This group of causal factors is inclusive of all those situations where the child is a screen on which a parent projects a compensatory fantasy that hinges on themes and personal problems which the parent has never resolved. Experiences of impotence, feelings of inadequacy, conditions of economic insecurity, and the frustrations that derive from the perception of belonging to a lower social class can all lead parents to hope to see their tarnished image redeemed by way of their child, and in their child. The child will never be loved for what he or she is, but for what he or she represents in the eyes of others; rewards will come in the wake of adapting to the models proposed; reproof will result from any failure to achieve the kinds of success desired; the child will be emotionally blackmailed on showing itself to be weak, incapable, or socially inept, or on displaying any other attitude that might be seen as an indication of its parents' inferiority. When a child is raised on the basis of models that derive from compensatory fantasies, father and mother superimpose an ideal image on the real boy or real girl and take no account of his of her individual characteristics, potential capacities or real desires. They fill the child with their own self-image as "parent and master," which is the negative face of the archetype, and the child entirely takes the brunt of it.

The real child, who by now no longer exists in the eyes of its father and mother, experiences the drama of occupying the space of another, at times the time of another, of living the life of another. The lack of underlying self-confidence and of a stabilized sense of the Self leaves the child with an interior emptiness, and with the need to find orientation always and only in the outside world. In constant, desperate, unreasoning search for an indication of what the other (generally a figure of authority) wants from him or her, the child is ready to adapt to any request at all, in order to maintain the relationship and the illusory sensation of security and love. The personality comes to be structured in terms of a "false self" (Winnicott 1960) that slowly destroys, from within, the child's interior world. The child knows no such things as sensations, needs, and least of all desires of his or her own. Creative individuality is sacrificed, and the child progressively and ever more completely identifies with what Jung calls the *persona*: the component of the psyche with which we show ourselves in the word of social relationships. The *persona*, here, has been imposed upon the child by the group, and the child's evolution finds its denouement in total inhibition: in growth that lacks all vital enthusiasm, and all real desire.

Self-respect, as such, will be entirely non-existent, and will depend on constant reconfirmation by the outside world. Autonomous growth and appropriate expression of libido and aggression seem to menace the integrity of the personality, and are also experienced with a great sense of guilt, since the child perceives that its false identity must also be maintained in order to create no crisis in the psychic structure of the adult with whom he or she is so intimately interconnected. The child cannot even think of itself as an independent being, since the very idea would already create a separation, a gap that would cause the loss of fusion with the other. The area of intellection is also compromised: extreme anxiety in the face of requests for achievement will provoke disturbances in symbolization, difficulties in learning, and finally the abandon of schooling: this set of symptoms is in fact quite common among children who are chronically exposed to stressful demands.

All normal processes of identification are here profoundly disturbed – since the threatening quality of the outside world allows no interiorization of role models – and the child's only option is an imitative mode of behavior that adheres to programmed models, and which thus assures the cohesion of the Self, but not its integration into a living, individual structure. The child perceives socialization to be dangerous – just like play and recreation, which are often opposed by the parents, who see them as a waste of time – and carefully avoids it, since there's too great a risk in any confrontation with anything different from what's known to deliver security and continuity: the risk of the total collapse of the false self. The presentation of a clinical case can offer a clearer understanding of how such pathologies evolve.

Marco is sixteen years old, and has the dark skin and typical facial features of a South American Indio. He's tall and strong, but seems stooped down around himself as he enters the studio. He's accompanied by his mother, who is a white European woman, quite advanced in age, and visibly charged with anxiety. She's looking for help since her son no longer wants to go to school. He no longer obeys her at all, and when she attempts to force things from him, he grows very angry and at times has even struck her. The family lives in a small town just outside of Rome, in the rural belt that surrounds the city, and Marco's father, whose age is even greater than his mother's, has land that he farms on his own. The couple had had no children and on filing an adoption request were told that they had passed the maximum consented age for adoptive parents. They had turned at that point to an international agency that offers solutions that circumvent such laws. The mother spent a month in Bolivia, where she registered a newborn Indio baby as her own. The child had been abandoned by his mother shortly after birth. The adoptive mother then returned with her child to Italy.

To understand this mother's perseverance – avoiding, as well, all attribution of guilt – we have to take a look at her personal history. She too had been abandoned at birth, and had grown up in an orphanage. She had left the orphanage on coming of age, but felt lost and nowhere at home in the outside world and had married the first man she met. He was a great deal older than she was, but had shown her affection and given her security. Her great aspiration was to redeem her own unhappy childhood through a child whose life might realize all the things of which she herself had been deprived. All the better if that child too had been abandoned at birth, since this was the condition she herself had known. She identified with a kind of savior complex, and had brought Marco up in an atmosphere of constant requests for achievements that quieted her anxious need for redemption of her social status. She drove him ahead in scholastic performance, and imposed ever more comprehensive restrictions on his world of play and social life; he wasn't allowed to see children his age outside of school, and sports were likewise prohibited. The boy, moreover, in the rural context in which he lived, was looked upon with curiosity, and at times with mistrust, by the other children around him. They remarked on his strange features and dark skin, and the fact that he took no part in the normal activities of his schoolmates surely did nothing to improve his already strained relationship with the other children. Every now and then Marco had asked his mother why he had darker skin than the others, and if this was the reason why they spent no time with him, but she had never treated his questions seriously, and had never told him the truth.

On reaching puberty, Marco was no longer willing to accept no more than his mother's generic chatter, and she was forced to reveal that he had been born in Bolivia, that his biological mother had abandoned him, and that she herself had adopted him at birth. The boy experienced a period of profound depression, and began to fantasize about his birth, his country of origin, and most of all his natural mother. He decided to return to Bolivia, in hopes of finding her, as soon as he came of age. This decision threw his mother into great alarm, and she began to reprove him, for ingratitude, saying, "I never had anything out of life, and I have given you everything. How can you think to go off on a hunt for the woman who abandoned you?" Marco began to do badly at school, and just barely managed to finish junior high school; and at that point he wanted to sign up for a vocational school that would allow him quickly to find a job, and to earn a little money with which to depart, as soon as possible, for South America. His mother, trapped in her anxieties and blinded by ideals that made her entirely insensitive to her son's requests, enrolled him at the high school for classical studies in Greek and Latin, where Marco promptly failed. This was the start of the worst period between the two, with the father entirely marginalized and incapable of helping the boy. He did, however, propose that Marco could help him with farm work. This was something the boy was happy to do, but which threw him into even deeper conflict with his mother's high academic demands.

This was the family's psychological situation when Marco accepted the idea of entering therapy. At the first session, he seemed seriously depressed, but after showing surprise at a request "to play with dolls," he constructed the scene in Figures 1 and 2.

Figure 1

It's immediately clear that the boy felt the need to delimit the field in which he worked by means of a fence that marked off an area in which he placed a house and a couple of horses, one of them mounted by a man, as well as a number of other animals and a few small trees. Outside of this corral, he placed a tractor, driven by a Playmobile figure. This is the scene as seen from my direction, but if we move into Marco's position and regard it from his point of view (Figure 5) we find a woman in front of the house along with a baby boy who's extending his arms toward his mother; and on the roof of the house there's a little elf-like devil (a "smurf" figure).

Figure 2

This was Marco's comment:

This is the house where I live. That's my father on the tractor, the woman is my mother, that's me when I was small, there are also horses and other animals. The man on the horse is a person who knows how to handle horses, but I don't know who he is.

I drew his attention to the fact that there also seemed to be another figure on the roof of the house, and, laughing like a small child, he told me that that was a little devil, and that he had put him there as a joke, then continuing that he could remove this figure if I wanted him to. I told him to leave it where it was, since perhaps that little devil held the solution to his problems. Without knowing, it, Marco in fact had activated the archetypal figure of the "Trickster," a divine rogue who's present in the mythology of many cultures, even at quite some distance from one another. Jung himself included a chapter on the Trickster in *Archetypes and the Collective Unconscious* (CW, vol. 9, part I). This mythological character, ambiguous and anomalous, a proteiform clown who mediates between men and the gods, also plays the role, involuntarily, of a demiurge. He provokes enormous disruptions in ordinary reality, but with the unintended result of remodeling human perceptions of reality, which in general is defined too narrowly, and mainly in terms that serve social purposes. The Trickster leads to a new and more creative bias on the part of the consciousness of the individual. And by way of the unknown personage who knew how to govern horses, the scene the boy had created spoke yet again of the possibility of a favorable direction of evolution; but even if individual, it was still a question of something potential, entirely unconscious, and with no indication of a concrete route toward its realization. Marco was willing to enter psychotherapy, and treatment proceeded for the first few months at the verbal level, since he rejected the notion of "playing games."

In three months of sessions, Marco told me his story, describing the anguish and disappointment of learning that he had been adopted; but he spoke above all of the pain of knowing himself to have been abandoned. We also discussed his plans to go to Bolivia as soon as he turned eighteen. In spite of his rigid upbringing, he was fond of his adoptive mother and father, and he understood that their decision to adopt him had relieved him of a situation which at best would have been highly precarious. These affections, however, weren't as strong as his longing for the original dyad which in fact he had never experienced.

After three months of analysis, Marco asked spontaneously if he could make another sand construction (Figure 6). He began it as before by constructing a fence around a house, but then the space inside the fencing seemed to have exploded. The space outside the fence held all sorts of confused and bizarre situations of which the corral, apparently, had no longer been able to contain the pressure. Inside the corral, nothing vital seems to have remained. There's a birthday cake with some candles, but no people. Outside the enclosure, by now defunct, are numerous scenes of combat between men and animals, and a variety of bizarre details, like the witch and the pig on the tree at the upper left. But in the midst of this image of cataclysm, with manifold scenes of violence, we also find, at the top and center, an Indian chief and a dark-skinned Playmobile figure who seem to talk quietly with one another.

Figure 3

Here's Marco's description of his scene:

There has been a catastrophe; the house has been destroyed; everywhere around there are wars and conflicts.

Again, just as on the first occasion, I drew his attention to an element of transformation which he himself had overlooked, and asked him for the story of the two people who appeared to be conversing so quietly with one another. He told me that they represented a boy who was asking for advice from an old wise man. The sand construction seemed to outline a dangerous situation; the cake with the candles was a warning that Marco's eighteenth birthday might plunge his life – and not only his – into catastrophic derangement, if something weren't done to reduce the tensions in the environment. But, again, there's that fragment at the top, where the dark-skinned boy and the old, wise man converse with one another: it seems to be a center that's capable of promoting psychic stability. This scene might easily be taken for a representation of the transference, but any such interpretation would be reductive; the scene, in fact, goes a great deal further than the personal transference relationship, since the image appears to hold Marco's access to a transpersonal dimension. The representation of the therapeutic relationship through the use of such specific characters – a dark-skinned boy and a Native American medicine man – is indicative of Marco's need to reconstruct his history and to reconnect with his roots as a Native American, but it also speaks of the ability to achieve this goal through a reconstruction of the relationship at the level of transpersonal archetypes, without the need to pursue it on more material terms. This representation was the only factor of stability in a scene that might otherwise be read as a harbinger of catastrophe.

At this point it seemed important to agree upon a plan with Marco's parents, and especially with his mother. Marco chose to attend an agricultural training school, and his mother accepted his decision, in spite of the very great pain of relinquishing her inflated fantasies. For a while the boy continued therapy, but then, in order to pursue his studies, decided to interrupt the sessions, even while remaining occasionally in touch with the therapist. He graduated, continued to work with his father, and, naturally, didn't go back to Bolivia in search of his past: though distant in time and real space, it had the psychological presence of an always active archetype.

The New Forms of Violence

The "new" forms of violence also include the various forms of "institutional" violence, meaning all those forms of abuse which are due to errors and shortcomings on the part of the various agencies which in some one way or another are entrusted with dealing with children and their problems, from the public health care centers to the agencies manned by social workers, from the schools to the juvenile courts. We're faced with an "institutional abuse" whenever one of these institutions doesn't fulfill its duties, or instead does something which it should not do. To give a few examples, an abuse of this type is committed by the doctor who needlessly sends a child to a hospital; or by the social worker whose fears prevent house visits, or, on the other hand, who makes them far too often, driven by a personal, persecutory ideology; or, again, by the classroom teacher who refuses to "waste time" at school with a retarded child, since that's what the special back-up teacher is there to do. There are also cases where juridical structures commit institutional abuses, issuing hasty orders and ill-considered decisions, or failing to set up adequate protective measures, or postponing decisions in situations of risk or certified abuse.

Many of these conditions seem to have come together in the case of David, in addition to the problems connected with his birth into a highly problematic family.

David had just turned six years old when he was accompanied to our clinic by a social worker at the foster home where he lived. The staff at the home complained that David was hyperactive, completely uncontrollable at school, aggressive and violent in both word and action toward schoolmates as well as to adults, especially to girls and women. At school he had grossly insulted his teacher, and the principal wanted to expel him. He had been housed already in three institutional foster homes before being sent to the one in which he lived at present. At the current home, he had finally found a male social worker with whom he had established a somewhat more stable emotional relationship, and that was the person who brought him to the first visit.

David's mother and father were both drug addicts, and both very young. His mother, in addition to using drugs, was also a small-time pusher, and was often arrested, periodically spending a part of her time in jail, until finally deciding, when David was three, to move to another area where no one knew her, and where she could go about her dealings more easily. She left the boy with his father, under the quite bland supervision of the SERT public social services for problems of drug addiction. There were also two other children, younger, who were likewise in the care of their father, and in part of their maternal grandparents and of one of their mother's sisters.

When the boy was four years old, his father began to abuse him sexually, and this came to the knowledge of the SERT social services. David was removed from his father's custody and began his itinerary among the institutions, while his mother's father and other members of her family began a legal battle for custody and/or adoption. Meanwhile, in the midst of a combination of hesitations on the part of the juvenile courts and an objectively difficult legal situation, full of subtleties that tremendously bloated the time required for reaching decisions, the boy was placed in an institution along with one of his sisters, from whom he was later separated when its directors ceased to be willing to keep him, owing to his violent behavior. David was then transferred to a public foster home, but here again he was quickly expelled, after only a few months, because he refused to obey all rules and would beat up the other children. His subsequent transfer to another home made things no better, since his behavior continued to be very violent. A further transfer to his current home seemed slightly to have changed the situation, since he was able to establish an affective relationship with a male social worker, and this allowed his observance of more socially acceptable behavior. Still, however, he could not tolerate rules, or any degree of frustration; his behavior was highly reactive, and he rapidly burst into violent, destructive episodes of acting out. He was particularly incapable, moreover, of accepting female figures in positions of authority, which made school a trial for all concerned. His school, like most elementary schools, had an almost entirely female staff.

Figure 4

At our first meeting, David presented himself as a very bright boy with dark, lively eyes. He was also neglectful of his clothing and personal cleanliness, and spoke with a heavy, regional accent, rounded out with curses and a plethora of four-letter words. He entered "the sand room" with a tough-guy air, holding in his hand a six-inch fingernail file as though it were a knife; showing it to me, he spoke with the tone of an adolescent bully and threateningly asked, "You got a kid?" I told him to take a look at the shelves where there were all sorts of kids, and to choose the one he liked the most. He chose a baby Jesus and took it into his hands, as though in place of the fingernail file, which he put back into his pocket; and he began at that point, quite surprisingly, to behave like a normal child his age, laughing at the toys and showing surprise as looked at them, poring through the materials on the shelves, and observing them enthusiastically. While continuing always to hold the baby Jesus in his hands, he constructed the scene in Figure 4.

He began by setting up the house and placed the kneeling Madonna before it. Then he searched quite frantically for something on the shelves. After a while, I asked if I could help him find what he was looking for, and he told me he was look-ing for God. I smiled as it passed through my mind that in his situation God alone could help him, and together we searched for a suitable figure. Careful inspection of the dolls led him to select a puppet that seemed to be a good representation of his idea of God: a walking figure with a staff, a white beard, and a lantern in his hand. He put it beside the Madonna and put inside the house the baby Jesus which till now he'd continued to hold in his hands. In front of the house he set up a phalanx of angels and shepherds. Then he chose a large lioness, with a ferocious face, as well as a crocodile and placed them in front of the house. Their backs were turned to the other figures, but their faces were directed toward the house. Immediately afterwards he started to set up a large number of soldiers in a half circle around the two animals, saying: *There have to be more of them, lots and lots of them, can't you see how strong those animals are?* Having finished setting up the soldiers, he arranged the stalls next to the house, but in such a way that one couldn't enter them, since the entrance was blocked by having been turned against the edge of the sandbox, so much so that David had to remove the roof of the stalls in order to be able to set up a family of cows inside it. Finally, next to the stalls, he set up the figure of a woman who was drawing water from a well.

Once he had finished the construction I asked him to tell me what he had represented, and he began to tell me a story.

A child has been born, but two monsters want to kidnap him, and to rip out his heart; in fact once already they managed to capture him, but they didn't have time to rip out his heart, because the soldiers arrived and saved him. Now the two monsters are trying again, and it's not so sure the soldiers will be able to hold them off.

I asked him if there was something we could do to help this child, and David, after thinking for a while, continued his story.

You know what we'll do? We'll take the child and hide him in the middle of the cows inside the stalls, and here instead of the real child we'll put a fake one, so that even if these two monsters manage to steal him and to rip out his heart, it won't make any difference to us, because he's a fake.

As he was telling me his solution, he in fact took the child he had chosen at first and hid it among the cows, placing another in the house as a substitute for it. As he left the room, he asked if he could return and play again another time.

It's clear that David, without at all being aware of it, had used his metaphorical story as a way of recounting his true story. But his construction in the sandbox had also shown many other things. His pain derived from a loss of all relationship with protective parent figures. The boy, instead of being cared for by a father and a mother, had found himself with a life that had turned his parents into a pair of monsters that wanted to rip out his heart. The parent archetypes had shown their terrible faces at far too early a stage, and had left him in a situation of intolerable anguish, fearing to be destroyed. His need to defend himself, and indeed to survive, had led him to effect a split in both his mother figure and his father figure. Whereas the terrifying aspects of both these archetypes are clearly present and active in the scene, the Good Mother has been transformed, regressively, into a stall full of cows, and has also been fully cut off from the rest of the psyche: for the time being, she remains inaccessible. The Good Father has been turned into an ideal image, divine, but entirely without protective power, as confirmed by the need for the intervention of a group of anonymous soldiers – perhaps the social workers – in order to save the boy from the monsters. The child in need of care and protection had also been hidden away in the stalls. A split in David's inner world has allowed the good child to remain in the company of the maternal spirit, but there are no doors through which to enter the place in which they live, and to reappropriate their relationship. And on the other hand, one clearly sees a defensive identification with the forces of aggression, which was David's technique for trying to survive in such a frightening and hostile reality. The ego, in isolation from the Self (Neumann 1990), has lost its *soul* and identifies with the negative hero which it holds in high regard for its violent and forceful modes of exterior and social behavior. The only chance for returning to health and wholeness lay in the possibility of recreating relationships between all these conscious and unconscious complexes into which the boy's psychic reality had splintered. It was indispensable for David to recover a relationship with the positive maternal figure that here took the form of the cows in the stalls, to rehumanize the father figure, and to reconnect with the real child, who was still alive but far too frail and vulnerable for any further contact. Only this profound reconstruction of healthy, normal relationships, which are necessary for adequate individual growth no less than for social development, could allow him perhaps to repair, though not to obliterate, the suffering that was threatening to destroy his capabilities of loving and being loved.

Stefano Marinucci

References

Jung, C. G (1959) *Archetypes and the Collective Unconscious* CW, vol. 9, part I, Princeton: Princeton University Press.

Marinucci, S. (2003) *Uno spazio per esistere*, Bergamo: Moretti e Vitali.

Neumann, E. (1990) *The Child*, Boston: Shambala.

The Self and Family Archetypes in Children

Francesco Montecchi

1. Realization of the Self and the Family Archetype

Within the various analytic models, the term "Self" has various meanings. This fundamental concept of Jungian psychology will here be understood to imply:
− a unifying principle;
− the initial moment of psychic and physical life;
− the driving force of the process that leads to the realization of the Self as goal-destiny-individuation.

In describing how the Self finds manifestation in the context of child development, I will start with the theories of Jung, Fordham and Neumann. The process of the activation and realization of the Self will then be illustrated by a number of sandplay images constructed by abused girls in the course of therapy. Analysis of these images will reveal how the damaged psyche can heal.

A reflection on the role of the Self in the childhood processes of maturation and transformation will also attempt to bring to light the central function of the parent archetypes and, above all, of what I have termed the "family archetype"

(Montecchi 1997a), which consists of the father-mother-child triad. As an inner family model, the family archetype – which exists from birth and is activated particularly in the oedipal phase – shapes the child's relationships with the internal and external family, and lays the basis of the needs and behavior of the future adult.

Born of clinical experience, as demonstrated by the sand-play images to which I will be referring, the hypothesis of the existence of a family archetype – which requires still further theoretical reflection and clinical assessment – seems to me to offers a theoretic bridge to other psychological models (from psychoanalysis, especially as applied to children and groups, to relational theories) and to the findings of the most recent research on children, with emphasis on the relational models in the collective unconscious and on the relational function of the Self.

2. Roots of Individual Development in the Jungian Model

Jung believed that every individual has a unique task of self-realization. From the moment of birth, the individual is in possession of an interior heritage of unconscious contents with which consciousness, willingly or not, must come to terms. The contents of consciousness are influenced and organized by the collective unconscious and do not exclusively depend on the action of the individual context (Jung 1928-1931, 1935-1954). The hypothesis of an unconscious project that needs to be fulfilled is widely supported by the post-Jungians. To illustrate how this process comes to manifestation, Marie Louise von Franz (1967) uses, for example, the metaphor of mountain pine trees. In a pine forest, the trees all look the same, but none are exactly alike.

In a latent form, the seed of a mountain pine tree contains the whole tree of the future, but each seed falls, in its own time, in a particular place, characterized by various special factors […]. The wholeness of the pine tree, which is latent in the seed, reacts to these circumstances […] so that the future development of the tree is clearly outlined. (ibid., page 162)

This is a clear metaphor of how every individual human being, from child to adult, has the innate tendency to realize a complete project, specific for each individual, which is organized around the center that regulates the life of the individual: the Self.

The realization of the Self constitutes a developmental process that makes man "that certain single being that he is" (Jung 1928). According to Jung (1909-1949, 1939-1954), the child at birth is no *tabula rasa* on which everything remains to be impressed, but a complex entity, individually determined. Already at birth, children are in possession of many things which they have never acquired but carry within themselves in the form of systems organized in a specifically human way, as parts of the collective unconscious.

In particular, the unfolding of the Self guides all the various components of development: motor, affective, cognitive, biological, etc. If we consider, for example, motor development, we note that children already possess within themselves the program of the motor models that they are ready to activate – with no need to learn them – thanks to environmental activation. Sucking, walking, and sexual activity are, in fact, innate activities that require no learning.

Through this and other observations from the biological context, we can recognize that, from conception, the child has a program of individual development, which following birth can be realized in actual life through the family, social and cultural realities with which he or she comes into contact.

Statements on child development in the work of Jung are few but fundamental, and were later expanded by a number of post-Jungians. Jung's notion of the course of development which the Self undertakes was further developed and particularized in Fordham's theory of the primary Self (1944-1969) and in Neumann's theory of centroversion (1949, 1963).

These authors elaborated an archetypal model of child development based on clinical material from analytical work with children, or with the "inner child" of adult patients. In the last few decades, the observation of infants has provided an opportunity to verify and closely examine their theories. Borrowed from the Kleinian world and theorized by Ester Bick (1964), the observation of infants has made it possible to re-read birth and child development in terms not only of personal but also of archetypal experiences. Further knowledge and confirmation have also been provided by other recent research into infancy, and, in particular, by the research of the Lausanne group, under the direction of Daniel Stern (1985, 1995).

Fordham was a precursor of the research which was later to investigate the psychic life of the fetus. Emphasizing the inborn features of the child, he (1944-1969) considers the individual and the individual's course of development to be only a single thing, and independent of the surrounding context. He recognizes the autonomous structure of the childhood psyche and the existence of an "a priori," which he identifies in the primary Self which exists prior to birth, and which is endowed with archetypal psycho-physiological potential: this is the basis of the inborn propensity for individuation.

The primary Self establishes the project of the child's psychic and physical maturation, which already makes the child a separate individual from the mother, even while still continuing to live inside her. In as early as the period of fetal life, the child is endowed with structures that will constitute the basis of his or her inner life. Among these structures, those concerning the parent figures are of particular importance to psychic development. Though influenced and activated by the real parents, the parental models are structured by their respective archetypes.

According to Fordham (ibid.), the parents' task is to limit themselves to the role of supporting the process of the maturation of the Self, since any psychopathology they may have could bring about deviations in the child's natural development.

The primary Self exists from the moment of conception. Prior to birth, the child is in a state of total integration, under the dominion of the archetype of the positive Great Mother. Returning to Jung's description of consciousness (1910-1946) as emerging from the unconscious like an island from the sea, Fordham sees the ego and the archetypes to derive from the ability of the child's primary Self to separate into parts. He defines this process as "deintegration." At birth, the Self deintegrates by dividing into opposites, and then reintegrates thanks to the diligence and appropriateness of the mother's care. The deintegration of the Self, which reoccurs in moments of distress and need such as hunger, cold, etc., allows the child to experience the negative pole of the maternal archetype, which alternates with the positive. But by soothing the child's discomfort, maternal care helps the Self to reintegrate, allowing the child to experience the unified bipolarity, positive and negative, of the archetype (Fordham 1944-1969; Sidoli, 1989).

The primary Self can be represented by symbols. In children, representations of the Self are rooted in the body image which is constructed on the basis of maternal care. Formation of the body image is thus the source of awareness of the Self, and also of the discovery of the inner and outer world.

Linked to the archetype of the parents, the primary Self directs, guides and controls the emergence of the ego and activates the passage from one archetypal structure to another.

This innate, compelling and goal-directed tendency of the psyche was also recognized by Neumann (1949), who called it "centroversion," and he also gave the name of "automorphism" to the drive which is present in children from birth to realize their own individuality within the collective context. Centroversion is the inborn aspect that orients the child's development and which, contrary to Fordham's assertions, acts in synchrony with the environmental stimulation mediated by the mother, whose task is to constellate the archetypal field and evoke the primal maternal image which is present in the child's psyche.

According to Neumann, the concomitance of the work of the Self and of environmental stimulation permits the unfolding of the structure of the archetypes, so that the dominance of one archetype is gradually replaced by that of another. To become psychically operational, the constellation of the archetypes needs to be evoked in ways which are appropriate for the child's particular phase of development, and initially they must be activated by real experience. The Self prepares and guides the meeting with the archetypes of the mother and then the father, and its energy gives a form to the child's perception of his or her parents (Jung 1909-1949).

At birth, the Self is rooted in the biopsychic unity of the body. The physical Self, as defined by Neumann (1963), contains physical and psychic identity, as well as heredity and individuality, within a single structure, and represents the first valid experience of the Self; the maternal Self, on the other hand, is the externalized and relational Self, and by finding its completion and complement in the physical Self of the child, it leads to a unitary Self.

In order to reach his or her own Self, the child needs to make use of the maternal Self for about one year after birth, in correspondence with the time required for learning how to walk.

When this "dual union" dissolves and the ego is born, a particular relation is established between the ego and the Self, the Ego-Self axis, in which the child has internalized the experience of the maternal Self. The basis for the healthy birth and development of the ego is the establishment of an adequate Ego-Self axis. The contrary happens when mothering is inadequate, providing either too little or too much care, which leads to a splitting in the evocation of the archetype of the Great Mother, and thus to the activation of a dominance of the Terrible Mother or the Good Mother.

If the Terrible Mother dominates, the ego will find its controlling structure in anguished feelings of frustration and abandonment. If the Good Mother dominates, adequate development will be obstructed and the child will be prevented from separating from her, owing to lacking integration of the negative side of the Great Mother (Neumann 1963). This situation is often described in myths and fairy tales. For example, in the story of Hansel and Gretel, as Neumann too recalls (1949), the child-devouring witch has a house made of candied fruit and marzipan.

During development, the child's Self is incarnated in the archetype that corresponds to the developmental phase. The Self holds the ego in continuous tension between the archetype it is urged to leave and the archetype towards which it is thrust. This developmental movement is favored and accentuated by the dual aspect, good-terrible, that characterizes the archetypes. In this way, the archetype of the previous phase, which assumes a restraining function, shows itself in its aspect of bringing terror and fear, while the next archetype shows its positive aspect (Neumann 1963).

The intuitions of Fordham and Neumann, though they were not without their differences, allowed them to delineate a Self that exists before birth and to see it as the source of the inborn tendency for individual development, and as such they were forebears of the kinds of research which the fields of genetics and the neurosciences developed for the study of the psychic life of the fetus.

Although many scientists who are concerned with the search for the biological roots of the emotions of the human soul feel that the theoretic presuppositions of psychoanalysis have been surpassed by recent discoveries in genetics, molecular biology and neurotransmitters, it is surprising to note that the theoreticians of analytical psychology have had intuitions which not only are not anachronistic, but which indeed have anticipated biological discoveries, thus making the meeting and cross-checking of biology and psychology now possible.

The identification and localization on the chromosomes of the so-called "candidate genes" – their name derives from the importance they hold in determining transmittable behavioral and pathogenic traits that relate to the individual's inborn heritage, and which are capable of giving orientation to the individual's specific project of development – might lead to the hypothesis that the biological site of the Self lies in the individual's DNA. Nurturing these aspects may help us perhaps to understand, and in part to control, what we now call "innate predisposition," "fate" or "destiny."

The next one hundred years will probably witness an explosion of knowledge regarding neurotransmitters and the genetic mechanisms at the basis of psychological types and of various aspects of psychology and psychopathology. Such knowledge will also have an influence on the theoretic and therapeutic models of psychoanalysis. Looking towards the future, we can imagine that it won't be possible for tomorrow's analysts to refrain from aligning their work with the neurobiological profile of the individual, thus integrating the concept of the Self with aspects of genetics that intertwine with environmental factors and subjective experiences. New models of analysis, guided by the knowledge of the genetic makeup of the individual, will be able to perceive and encourage the development of potentials and maximum autonomy, and to do so without any reference to the Self as an abstract entity, in isolation from biological and genetic fact.

After this digression into biology, and after recalling the model of the Self proposed by Fordham and Neumann, I will now return to Jung's ideas, and to various considerations on the course of child development.

3. Stages of Development and the Activation of the Archetypes

Jung's theory of the archetypes sees two factors in a state of constant tension: an instinctive factor that also holds the beginnings of sexuality, and a spiritual factor that corresponds to the higher mental and spiritual functions.

In the first stage of development, the child becomes aware only of the instincts that find their basis in the various stages of bodily awareness (oral, anal, phallic, etc.) and in the factors that work against it (Jung 1928b). In his further development of Jung's theoretical hypothesis, Neumann (1949) elevated the body and its body language to the status of an archetype. The dominance of the physical Self and of the instinctive pole of the archetypes, especially in the early stages of development, explains why the body is the child's main channel for the expression of emotional contents, which are experienced as both positive and negative. The body is also the channel for the expression of emotional distress, which explains the frequency of psychosomatic manifestations.

Body language later becomes the root of the development of the contents of the psychic world, feelings and thoughts, and permits the passage from the bodily to the mental. The bodily model of ingestion-vomiting, spitting, etc. returns in the course of the various developmental stages, leading up to the achievement of the mental model of introjection-projection.

The swallowing-spitting, digesting-vomiting, withholding-evacuating, grasping-throwing model constitutes the first way in which children accept what they feel to be good (milk = love) and reject what they feel to be bad, negative, indigestible, smelly, unacceptable.

What is removed, projected or evacuated in a closed, hidden place also provides the first occasion for the child's contact with the shadow, which finds its incarnation in the indigestible, unacceptable, intolerable, negative. This activation of the shadow, already present from the first months of life, is similar to the paranoid-schizoid position described by Kleinian psychoanalysts (Zoja 1986).

The emergence of these archetypal experiences is particularly important at the time of learning to walk, which corresponds to leaving the maternal world. In this stage, the child sets out on a path of exploration, often with the guide of an exploring and intrusive finger.

Activity, motricity, exploration, aggressiveness, penetration, curiosity, and the desire for knowledge represent male contents; they are precursors of the male *logos* and the female *animus*, but derive archetypally from the experience of the mother.

If these first experiences of exploring and knowing are blocked or become too painful to be tolerated, the drive to learn, the epistemological instinct, may be repressed. Such repression also results in a decline in the capacity for scholastic learning, where refusal to learn and know is rooted in an ancient association between knowledge and pain (Montecchi 1995).

4. Representations of the Self

The self's peculiar features include the rational and irrational, empirical and transcendent, and can be made perceptible through symbol. The symbols of the Self that most frequently appear in our common stock of images are the old wise man, the helpful animal, wind, religious symbols such as the divine child, Christ, Buddha, etc., but also geometric figures such as the square and circle.

Fordham (1944-69) frequently noted that children often draw or paint geometric figures that correspond to those described by Jung as symbols of the Self. These generally circular figures are endowed with a center and a variable internal structure.

Circles can be symbolic of the total Self. Their appearance goes hand in hand with the development of the ego, which becomes capable of representing the Self in which it is contained. It is also possible to link these structures to experience of the body. The impenetrability of the circle can correspond to the primitive experience of parts of the body or to its total image. It can evoke the fertilized egg at the moment of conception, the eyes, the body's principal orifices, the maternal breast, which all have a circular form. There are numerous circular objects, available to infantile inspection, on which the total Self can be projected. Now I would like to deal with the representation of the Self in sandplay images constructed by abused girls. The choice of such images is motivated not only by the fact that the problem of child abuse is one of my principal areas of activity in hospital, but links above all to the observation that the traumatic experience of abuse, which represents a serious threat to the integrity of the Self, permits us to reveal both the innate vulnerability and the healing potential which are present in every abused child.

When the pain of an event in one's life is too intense, it results in the activation of numerous defense mechanisms which obstruct its elaboration. If, instead, the correct distance from suffering can be found so that the ego is not over-whelmed, and so that it is possible to feel, think and represent the pain, it becomes more bearable. The work of elaborating and representing, just as we see with many artists, transforms life itself into a sort of "work of art." Abuse and mistreatment provoke great suffering, and in doing so force the individual to the deployment of resources that can bring about healing (the "good" part of the personality) not only for self-defense, but as well for the "production" of increased humanity, thus also prompting the individual to become more sensitive and atten-tive both to him- or herself and to others.

4.1. Clinical Cases

The first case is a nine-year-old girl who along with a girlfriend was raped by a stranger while walking in the woods near Rome (Montecchi 1989). Ever since the time of her birth, her parents had been largely absent due to work, and her care had been entrusted to a sister who was seven years older. Nevertheless, the girl spent a lot of time alone in a three-story house.

In one of her first sandplay images, the girl placed various animals inside a circle drawn in the sand. This gesture was repeated whenever she felt the pressure of her instincts.

Figure 1

The image of the circle takes us back to the Self, which in this case is called upon to contain and guide the emergence of instinct. The magical omnipotence of the circle, which is present in many rituals, is also frequently deployed as a system of control. Bad, frightening objects can be placed inside a circle for the purpose of confining them: so that they can't get out. Or good, valuable objects can be placed inside a circle to protect them from external dangers, of an often catastrophic nature (Fordham 1944-69).

Now I will explore the details of an image constructed during one of the sessions. I have chosen this image because of the intensity of some of the contents it represents, and also because it brings to light a number of themes that are recurrent among children who have experienced a lack of parental affective care, previous to actual sexual abuse, as I have often observed in clinical practice.

The image was constructed in two stages: in the first, the girl set up houses, a fountain, and a few of the seven dwarfs; at the center she placed a boy playing ball, and in the upper right corner, an octopus. She described the scene as a town in which people work, "they hoe, spade and pick flowers, the boy plays," while the octopus threatens and blocks whoever passes by.

Analysis of this sandplay image reveals the workings of energies that act in the depths (the dwarfs), in spite of the constant threat, the ever-present obstacle, of a deadly maternal embrace (the octopus to the upper right). Though never mentioned verbally, it was represented.

Figure 2

In the second stage of constructing the image, the girl added a turtle in the center, two dolphins in a fountain, and a Madonna and child in the lower left corner, hidden by a house. "Back there, in secret, a baby is being born!" she said, thus revealing the emergence, even though secretly, and in opposition to the octopus, of a positive mother figure and a new birth. She then placed at the bottom a large fir tree with a man on it, saying, "That's a prince who looks at everything from above; he captured two dolphins and has put then in the fountain on his farm."

This image's other surprising element is the relation between the dolphins and the prince: there are two captured dolphins, just as two girls were captured and raped in the woods. Docile, frolicking mammals with strong family ties, dolphins are symbols that abused girls often use for docile femininity in transition. But their most distinctive characteristic in the collective imagination is that they are helpful animals. Their appearance signals the presence of the healing potential of the Self.

As announced by the sandplay image of the child being born in secret, therapy – which lasted for more than two years – helped this patient to find within herself the energy to be both mother and father to herself, and to overcome the unconscious conviction and tempting belief, which emerged frequently during the sessions, that being raped was her only way to be accepted, cared for and loved.

Another case is a severely depressed ten-year-old girl, daughter of an unwed anorectic mother who not only did not feed her, but who also gave her no affection (Montecchi 1997b). This woman, who lived by her wits and who was always in economic straits, used men as a way to earn a living, flanking her office work with a night-time job as an *entraîneuse*. The girl was often left alone at home, and for company she sometimes went to visit a neighboring elderly couple. It was the elderly man who abused her.

When she was referred to me at Bambin Gesù Children's Hospital in Rome, the girl was suffering from a severe lack of both physical and affective care. Betrayed by her need for affection, she had had to endure abuse from a person she considered a loving "grandfather," and whom now she had to testify against in court. There was also the risk – the possibility of a further loss – that the Juvenile Court would remove her from her mother's custody.

In the first sandplay images, the patient filled the scene with fierce animals, filling up all the empty spaces. For about three months, in subsequent sessions, her sandplay images unconsciously represented her mother's work and the numerous boy friends who came to their house, and they also referred to her accompanying her mother to the night club, so as not to have to remain at home alone.

One day, when she was particularly sad, she constructed a scene full of sweet foods and cooking utensils. Oral behavior was no longer acted out (as in the first session) by filling up empty spaces, but by representations of things to eat.

Figure 3

While observing this sandplay image, I directed my attention not only to the oral themes it represented, but also to the possibilities implied by kitchen utensils. It seemed that the girl was able to begin to elaborate affective nourishment on her own, and to experience the oral function as a instrument for the acquisition of knowledge.

The outline of the project announced in this scene appeared in more complete form in one of the final sessions, during which the girl constructed a sandplay image that divided into an upper part, representing an area of land, and a lower part, representing a stretch of water. In the water part, she placed a small boat with a female figure in it, two small fish, and a shark.

Figure 4

On the land she placed a horse, a tiger and a few plants. She moved the boat through the sand until it reached the land, where she removed the female figure from the boat.

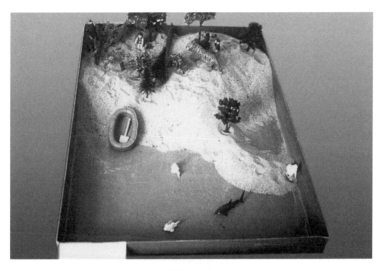

Figure 5

She commented on the sandplay image by telling a sort of fairy tale that recounted both her real and psychic story: *A little girl is left alone in a boat, a shark wants to eat her and circles around her, but she uses an oar to make him go away. She lands on an island where she finds a tiger that threatens her, but she meets a horse who loves her and who helps her to learn to avoid being attacked by the tiger, and how to build, all by herself, a hut in which she can live.*

She then placed a pelican on the right-hand side of the sandbox.

This image is self-explanatory, but comment can be made on its implications with regard to the transference, and of the appearance of threatening oral themes, as represented by the shark and tiger. The girl in the story can learn to make them harmless thanks to energies which are entirely her own, and activated by a good, helpful horse, which is an image of the analyst as well as of the healing aspects of the Self.

Figure 6

In the course of therapy, already previous to this session, the patient had developed an eroticized and seductive transference, surprising in a ten-year-old girl, through which she attempted to re-experience the erotic games of the "grandfather." The reinsertion of the traumatic experience into the transference showed multiple contents that appeared to be separate and contrasting. The erotic transference had the function of healing the wounds caused by abuse, but at the same time, the seductive behavior had the purpose of neutralizing therapy, which was felt to be a threat to her system of defenses. As well, the repetition of the trauma in the transference, and the deceptive affective advantage obtained by being a victim of abuse were also her way of expressing her need for a warm, accepting parent function.

Construction of this image was possible only after the acknowledgement of the different meanings expressed in the transference. Analysis of the image reveals the activation of a process of transformation. In trauma deriving from experiences of child abuse, normal processes of the humanization of the Self are interrupted. The Self remains archaic and often finds manifestation in the form of warring opposites. In scenes represented in dreams, drawings and sandplay images, defense against the kinds of distress which are activated by trauma finds its personification in archetypal images that portray the defense mechanisms which have been activated, the dissociative activities of the psyche, and as well the tensions toward the unification of psychic fragments. In this process, the personality of the individual can develop only if the energies preserved at deeper levels are freed and integrated. If the individual possesses interior energies that he or she can invest in the struggle, they can constitute a third and mediatory element between the two split-off parts: the most developed part of the ego thus takes care of the regressed part of the personality (Kalsched 1996).

In the production of fantasies, the regressed part can be represented by a child or a vulnerable animal that incarnates the indestructible core of the individual, also at the level of transpersonal content (the Self). The advanced part of the personality can be represented by an important benevolent or malevolent figure, depending on the nature of the real-life situation, that protects or persecutes the vulnerable part. Sometimes the benevolent and protective aspect is presented as a fantasy animal, as a special horse or dolphin, or at other times as a guardian figure. In still other cases, the benevolent-protective and malevolent-threatening aspects coexist.

The advanced and regressed parts are coordinated by the Self, which also includes an ambivalent (Jung 1951) "dark side" that is often experienced as destructive and negative (Schillirò 2000). This theoretical hypothesis can find support in our first sandplay image, where the shark and the tiger constitute the threatening side, while the wonderful horse represents the protecting element.

This image is also indicative of how the eroticization of relations and feelings finds incarnation in threatening animals, and of how the response of the analyst, accepting but not yielding to the transference's requests, has activated the girl's personal resources so that she is able to defend herself from threats, and to constellate an archetypal transference, as represented by the wonderful, loving horse that guides her, as well as by the pelican.

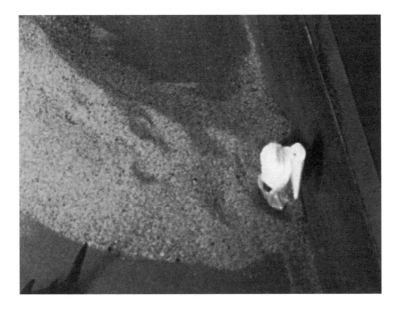

Figure 7

The helpful animal is a recurrent motif in fairy tales and myths. When it appears in the unconscious productions of an individual, it symbolizes instinctive nature in relationship with the environment, and can also be considered a representation of the Self. In *The Phenomenology of the Spirit in Fairytales*, Jung (1946-48) explains that helpful animals behave like human beings and speak in human language, but show knowledge superior to that of man. They also incarnate the archetype of the spirit, expressed in animal form.

Another poignant feature of this sandplay image is the presence of the pelican, which is a humble and not very solemn image of the Self. Some legends narrate that when there is no food, the pelican tears open its breast to nourish its young with its own blood. The pelican has thus become a symbol of parental love and, in Christian iconography, one of the symbols of Christ.

In *The Dream of the Virgin,* a painting in the Ferrara museum, dated approximately 1350, and analyzed by Jung (1944) in *Psychology and Alchemy,* a tree protrudes from the womb of the sleeping Madonna.

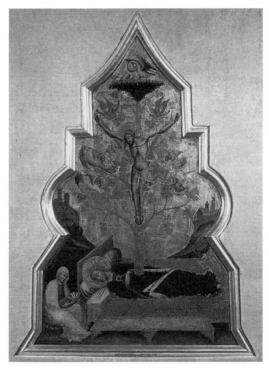

Figure 8

The painting shows Christ crucified on the tree, and at the top a nest in which a pelican is feeding its young with pieces of its own heart. Jung (ibid.) associates this image with a text on alchemy, the *Cantilena Georgii Riplaei*, which narrates the legend of a king who was born sterile. To become fertile he must return to the womb of his mother, associated with the Virgin Mary, and be reborn from her through the tree of Christ. In the image as well as in the comment, the pelican, which is often found in religious iconography, especially of the Middle Ages, seems associated with a process of transformation, of death and rebirth, that presupposes an activation of the Self and the parental archetypes.

The image of the pelican in the sandplay image has much the same content. The scene the patient represents shows how the process of transformation, experienced and represented through sandplay, has also constellated the deep, ancient healing energy that belongs to the Self.

The good instinctuality of the horse, an animal manifestation of the Self as well as a representation of an archetypal transference activated by the relationship with the therapist, now protects the girl from an archaic, threatening and devouring instinctuality – activated in its sexual aspects also by the experience of abuse – and from a terrible, deadly maternal figure, both represented by ferocious animals. The girl thus begins to free herself from the shortcomings of the maternal figure, which had exposed her to the negative aspect of the Great Mother archetype, as well as from the danger of a seductive, abusing male figure that could have imprisoned her in the net of a destructive *animus*. The male-spirit incarnated in the helpful horse shows the activation of the creative and self-healing aspects of the psyche. The appearance of the pelican shows how the archetypal parental function was constellated within the therapeutic setting, thus making up for the shortcomings of the real parental experience.

Through a new and positive experience of trust in the analytic relationship, the girl could start to repair the damage produced by her experiences, finding again the psychic space in which to carry out her own life project.

These clinical cases show how children's hands can narrate and elaborate inexpressible experiences in the "free" and "protected" space of the sandbox (Kalff 1966, p. 15). In handling the sand and positioning the objects within the sandbox to represent a scene, the patients' hands give form to problems that threaten them, to conflicts in their inner world, to real facts that cannot be revealed by words; but they also express the life project concealed within the folds of emotional distress (Montecchi 1993, 1997b).

5. The Family Archetype

The cases described here also reveal the importance of the archetypal parental function, and as well give indications of its connections with the Self. Attention to parent images and to unconscious family models has permitted me to broaden the scope of my reflections on the ways of representing and realizing the Self, and thus to develop the hypothesis of the existence of a family archetype, the role of which is of great importance in the unfolding of the Self, especially in children. I would like to illustrate this hypothesis through the presentation of a final clinical case, preceded by a series of theoretical considerations.

The Jungian school often refers to the mother and the maternal archetype, to the father and the paternal archetype, to the child and the child archetype, all of which are related to the Self, but it considers these figures separately. This theorization doesn't take account of the relationships between these three quite clearly inseparable figures: there cannot be a child if there is no father and mother, just as there can be no father or mother without a child and the other parent.

The union of these three figures, which are intimately interconnected and mutually essential to the developmental processes, constitutes an archetypal model that not only has the task of regulating family relations, but which is also closely related, by virtue of producing the integration of opposites, to the functioning of the Self.

The activation of the family archetype accompanies the entire life of the individual, structuring his or her relationships with the internal and external family, and assuming particular importance during the oedipal stage. Every individual experiences the family archetype from the moment of conception. The mother-father-child triad is biologically imprinted in our experience of the body, and constitutes the essence of all psychic dynamics, given the inseparability of the experience of the body from that of the psyche, and vice versa.

Psychoanalysis has greatly emphasized the role of the mother, both real and interior, in child development, with an exclusive, one-sided concentration on the mother-child relationship, relegating the role of the father only to a later moment. The non-scientific basis of such an approach, and its lack of conformity with clinical observation, has stimulated compensatory attention to the father, as exemplified by Luigi Zoja's *The Father* (2001). It has also led to the research of Elisabeth Fivaz-Depeursinge and the Lausanne group (Fivaz-Depeursinge, Corboz-Warnery 1999), which, through LTP (Lausanne Triad and Play), has offered experimental demonstration of the existence of a process of primary triangulation which constitutes the basis of the child's communication with both parents, from as early as the very first months of life. The authors have observed the way in which children already in the period immediately after birth alternate the direction of their gaze between the two parents: this is to say that starting already at the time of birth the child directs attention and affects in the direction of both parents.

In the early stages of development – as also occurs with the other archetypes – the family archetype is activated by way of the body. Exploration of their own bodies, and the concomitant acquisition of a personal image of the body, lead children on reaching the so-called phallic stage to discover their genitals, as well as the difference in general between the two sexes, and between mother and father in particular.

This stage culminates in the Oedipus complex, with the activation of incestuous desires. Jung (1913) considers the incest fantasy to be an archetype, of which the image conceals a symbolic meaning with dual content: regressive on one hand and progressive-transformative on the other.

Concern with the incest theme must take into consideration the point in the developmental process at which it is evoked, since its appearance is of different significance in children and adults. During the oedipal stage, the child prepares for a critical passage, from the physical to the spiritual, from the familial to the social and collective (coinciding with going to school). This passage is also perceived as a loss of a bond with the parents, and it activates a withholding drive that tends to entrench the psyche in the original bonds already experienced (Neumann 1949).

Incestuous desire also represents an attempt to remain anchored within the family, and it speaks as well of the need for endogamic union in the service of the integration of the components of the psyche. From this point of view, incest symbolizes the tendency to the union of homogeneous forms, the exaltation of the individual's own peculiar essence, and the discovery on the part of the individual of his/her own profoundest depths. Through effecting a union with his or her own being, past or future, the individual contributes to the intrapsychic process of individuation (Jung 1946), where looking back at what is dying is no obstacle to moving forward, and the result is that life can be lived with greater intensity (Jung 1912-1952).

Oedipus and the incest archetype are experienced through the real parents, who acquire psychic significance not only because of the care they bestow on the child or owing to the processes of attachment, but also because of their incarnation of archetypal models. These models are present in the child as a part of the child's inborn heritage, and though requiring the presence of the real parents for their initial activation, they would continue to be active even in the event of their death (Jung, 1916-1948; Neumann 1963). In addition to the real parents, the parent *imagos* are very important.

Although the oedipal triangle is often considered to be problematic, owing to the conflictuality it triggers in the child's relationship with his/her parents, it is also a family triangle that guides the child towards a more integrated and no longer separate activation of the maternal, paternal and child archetypes. It is precisely this capacity to effect integration that binds the family archetype to the Self, one of the principal functions of which is to integrate psychic opposites through synthesis by way of symbol.

One of the pairs of opposites which the Self contains is the male-female, of which the first expression refers to the parental couple. From an endopsychic point of view, the tension that drives a man and woman to unite and generate a child expresses the need of the male-female pair to reach a superior unity, creating a third element that synthesizes the given opposites at a level of greater integration. As a psychic image, the child corresponds to and incarnates the parents' needs for integration and development, representing the energies and new possibilities produced by a union of opposites (Baldassari, Bufacchi 2000).

The tension towards integration which characterizes the parent couple permeates the entire family triad, inclusive of the corresponding psychic movements of the child toward the parents. Within the oedipal situation, the tension between attraction and opposition to the parent figures activates the transcendent function, which integrates opposites and connects the unconscious and conscious, thus permitting the emergence of a third reality from the resolution of polar opposites.

Attraction to the parent of the opposite sex and rivalry with the parent of the same sex is not the only pair of opposites activated. In addition to affects of opposing male or female sign, the child also experiences the male and female contents incarnated by the two parents, and these are contents which the child must acknowledge and integrate within himself/herself.

In the oedipal stage, the intrapsychic union of the male and females poles, represented by the parents, produces a third symbolic element – the family archetype – that promotes integration, including and summarizing all the oedipal dynamics.

Activation of the family archetype is subject to the same laws that regulate the constellation of all archetypes, which are activated, in real situations, when the child encounters persons who evoke and correspond to them. The developmental process of activating archetypes can also be partial, just as they can also be separate from the figures who evoke them.

The child's family *imago* is an inner representation that derives from the child's relationship with his/her parents. This *imago* only partly corresponds to the real family, from which it differs in various ways that depend on the personal needs of the child, or by virtue of features that appear to compensate for aspects which are missing or incomplete in the real family.

The activation of separate or missing aspects of archetypal images causes the compensatory emergence of the representation of the missing part of the archetype, and sometimes causes an idealization of the parent figures and the family triad.

If the external family situation is characterized by deficiencies and split-offs, and if the child attempts to realize the activation of the family archetype in real life, rather than giving it recognition as an inner need, the child will encounter growing frustration, which can turn into the root of profound distress. On the other hand, even if the family archetype is activated in a real condition of loss, absence and distress, acknowledgement of its status as an inner psychic reality that requires integration can liberate energies that foster the process of individuation, as happens, for example, in children whose parents are separated.

On shifting attention from children to adults, one notes that here again the family archetype can lie at the focus of any number of important problems that involve the life and behavior of the individual, and which gravitate around it. When adults attempt to realize, in real-life reality, the positive side of the family archetype, aspiring to an idealized family, their attempts are destined to fail, causing great dissatisfaction and suffering and rendering their affective relationships particularly problematic.

In cases such as these, analytic work can help the individual to acknowledge the family archetype as an endopsychic reality and as a representation of the Self, and thus to free up the energy which one has to have to be able to deal with the inevitable vicissitudes that accompany the formation of a real-life family.

6. Representations of the Family Archetype

The family archetype is found in every epoch and in every culture. In the western world, it also finds its manifestation in one of the most frequent images of Christian iconography, the Holy Family, and in the trinitarian representation of the divinity, which is the image that structures the whole of Christian theology. Whereas in the Holy Family we find a triad of mother, father and child (Mary, Joseph and Jesus), the Trinity is composed of Father, Son and Holy Ghost, which in Old Testament iconography often appears as female Wisdom (*Shekhinah*). In his comments on the dogma of the Trinity, which he saw as an expression of the Self, Jung (1942-1948) underscores the correlation between Mary and the Holy Ghost, whom the Gnostics saw as a mother.

The importance of the image of the Madonna, especially for Catholics, lies in more than revealing the importance of the female-maternal in a religious culture dominated by male aspects; more than anything else, it reveals the psychic need for the representation of a supernatural family triad that expresses the transpersonal aspect of the family model.

Turning from religious imagery to clinical experience, we note that the family archetype, which appears in the nativity scenes of Christian iconography, also makes frequent reappearance in the dreams, drawings, and sandplay images of many patients, especially children.

7. The Family Archetype in Analytic Therapy

To illustrate how the family archetype presents itself in the context of analytic therapy, I will turn again to a case of abuse encountered in my hospital work, since family bonds and the parental experience are severely damaged among such patients. The theme of the family archetype occurs very frequently in their sandplay images.

The case is a thirteen-year old adolescent with *anorexia nervosa* who was referred to the Psychiatric and Psychotherapy Unit of Bambin Gesù Children's Hospital in Rome (Montecchi 1997). Though she was also very thin, this girl was above all depressed, hypomimic and slow in speaking.

Her depression had begun in the wake of "impertinent" behavior by her father, such as touching and exhibiting his erection: behavior which in spite of great resistance she was able to describe in the course of therapy. As well, she did not feel accepted and protected by her mother, who was often away from home because of work. The girl was constantly waiting in disappointment for one or the other of her parents. Though aware of her sadness, she did not want to discuss it, since she was afraid that discussing it might increase it. Given her difficulty with talking, I suggested that she express herself through sandplay.

She constructed her image slowly and obsessively, placing a nativity scene in the lower right corner of the sandbox and the Three Wise Men in the opposite corner. She then added various animals and a house in the lower left corner. This is her description of what was taking place: *The people go to worship the Holy Child, bringing gifts, animals and food. The Three Wise Men are also there and are bringing precious gifts, but they are still far away and have a long way to walk. The Holy Child is there to receive these things; he doesn't think, he just accepts the gifts.*

Figure 9

I would like to point out the significant elements that appear in this sandplay scene. First, the Holy Child is outside, with no shelter, no container, and he is there only to receive gifts, mostly food. Oral themes are acted out in this image, and represented by gifts of food.

The triad of the Three Wise Men, which alludes to the Self, instead brings concrete gifts which are not food, and which lead to transformation. The Wise Men are also images of a paternal archetype, and represent transformative elements that are still too far away. In this sandplay image, however, the Holy Child is not associated with the themes of nativity, renewal, potential becoming, and new possibilities of development, but instead with regression and passivity, since he is there only to receive.

The role of this Holy Child recalls some of the treatments deployed against depression by the primitive medicine of some of the Native American tribes. Recovery came about as a result of the satisfaction of frustrated wishes, as revealed by dreams to the afflicted individual or the shamans. Therapy was carried out through "dream festivals," where, during the banquet, the members of the tribe brought the afflicted person things, or symbolic substitutes for things, they supposed that person desired. Thus, in symbolic form, the depressed patient regained the lost love object (Ellenberger 1970).

While revealing a severe psychic condition, this sandplay image also indicated the possibility of transformation. The creation within the sandbox of such a nativity scene was a sign of the activation of the family archetype that consists of the father-mother-child triad which in various forms would also reappear in later sandplay constructions.

When the psychic situation is centered, as here, on the relationship with the maternal principle, activation of the family archetype is very important, since it removes the relationship with the Mother from its central position and triggers in the patient a fantasy of rebirth, and of transformation of the inner family.

In the context of family therapy, which proceeded on a parallel with individual therapy, important psychic movements were taking place. The conflicts between the parents were emerging, after having in the past been carefully masked, and their appearance was driving the parents to consider the idea of divorce. These movements within the family group were accompanied by those of the girl's psyche, which at this point found itself faced with themes regarding the family.

During a session at the distance of a year from the start of therapy, the girl created a sandbox scene that represented "a family having their picture taken on the day of the parents' wedding anniversary." Just as in her own family, this family group contained four children. This similarity reinforced the connection between the real-life world and the inner world which was represented in the sandbox. In commenting on the anniversary photograph, the girl remarked: *This is a reminder that in marriage people stay together and don't separate.*

Figure 10

There was an obvious connection between what was happening in the girl's family and in the family sessions, and what was happening in her individual therapy, where the theme of the inner family was being activated and elaborated. The united and idealized family that she wished to see turn into a real-life reality was represented in the sandplay image since she was not yet able to recognize such an image of the family archetype as an inner need of her own. The presence of a photographer and the scene's reference to a photograph were clear indications of the attitude with which this inner reality needed to be viewed: the important thing would be to recognize its value as an image.

Whereas the photographer who can observe reality and transform it into image is an incarnation of the individual egoic function which is activated by therapy and the transference relationship with the therapist, the camera is an indication of

140

how this process could be carried out. Cameras view and focus reality through their diaphragm and lens, thus permitting the selection, isolation and focusing of what is to be impressed on their film, which then results in a printed photo that holds alive the memory of events which took place in the past.

The patient seemed involved in a process of selecting and focusing the family image which later she would hold within herself. The fact that it was a happily united family also revealed her need and capacity to hold the inner family image united within herself.

Sandplay therapy had started out with an image of a weak and non-cohesive family in which a passive child was a receiver of gifts (as seen in the first sandplay construction it had then moved on to an idealization of a united family (as represented by way of the image of a photograph of a wedding anniversary); and now, finally, in one of the last of the sandplay constructions, it had produced an image of an inner family that permitted and accompanied the patient's growth.

During one of the last sessions, the girl set up another nativity scene, again at the top of the box; there was also a well at the center of the box, a number of suitcases at the center right, and a cake with candles at the bottom. She described this image as "a nativity scene, but a special nativity, since there is no longer any need for others to come with gifts." The well too was very important, since at its bottom lay many "whys" and "desires." (Figure 11)

In the well "we sometimes look for treasures, but now we can find them and create them all on our own, with our own means and abilities." Looking at the suitcases, she exclaimed, "The suitcases! Who knows why I put them there? Maybe this is a station. They're probably getting ready to go somewhere."

Figure 11

This sand construction evidenced a project for change and the acquisition of autonomy. The nativity scene no longer represented a regressive and passive situation, but a possibility for development and renewal, perhaps a true rebirth, centered on the family triad. The family archetype had grown active within the girl, and was recognized as a potential source for the liberation of psychic energy.

The water at the bottom of the well, a necessary element for transformation, concealed a treasure: the potential energy on which the girl could draw without expecting solutions and protection to come from others.

The circle of candles that indicated a birthday was also a symbol of the passing of time: things that come and go were held in the notion of a year that ends, and of another that begins. On the one hand, the girl was preparing to separate from her real family, accepting its limits, and to entrust the planning of her inner family to the outside world, to her friends, and her first loves. On the other hand, this question of separation also concerned her therapy, which had achieved its goals. Celebration of rebirth could also include separation from the therapeutic relationship. The image of the suitcases – set up nearly unconsciously – and their association with a station and a coming departure seemed to leave no doubt. This sand construction was also an image of the making of plans for the end of therapy.

In fact, her therapy came to an end a few months later, with the full awareness that she did not have a normal home. Referring to her mother, she said, "She is what she is, and there's nothing I can do to make her any different." She remarked concerning her father, "I don't pay him any attention anymore, and there's nothing he can do to me. Now I am interested in my friends."

Aware of having to draw on her own energy, she no longer lay expectations in thoughts of a mother who might protect her, or of a father who loved, respected and appreciated her. She knew she could count on the inner family that had been activated during therapy; she knew she could find what she needed within herself. The reference to friends suggested an opening up to the outside world where perhaps she might one day be able to create a family of her own, different from the one into which she had been born: a family neither in shambles nor idealized, and with the capability of consciously facing up to problems and difficulties.

8. Activation of the Self and the Family Archetype as a Route to Psychic Transformation

In order to be able actually to effect a transformation, the constellation of the family archetype requires a lengthy course of psychic development that conducts the patient to a difficult confrontation with what Jung terms the "naked truth" (1946,

143

p. 243-252). Otherwise, such a transformation remains no more than an announced but never experienced possibility.

Analytic therapy can help a patient make contact with his or her psychic reality, guiding the individual through a project of personal development that finds its orientation in a transpersonal vision that prevents the individual from remaining entrapped in the painful events of his or her personal life. Understanding the archetypal model of existence can change the reading of such events and give a more positive turn to an individual's "destiny."

Though the model of the Self elaborated by Jung and the post-Jungians gives recognition, albeit with certain differences, to innate propensities and a kind of "predestination" in the developmental process, such predestination is not absolute. The inner model of the individual can in part be changed, and this, precisely, is the possibility that makes therapy meaningful. Analysis does not allow us to escape our psychological and biological destinies, but it enables us to give them a positive meaning (Bernhard 1969). Things can be changed if we understand our own model of existence and can thus avoid a number of its negative workings. In this way we can give a more positive turn to "destiny."

The ability to review traumatic events experienced in the course of childhood – events which are often associated with the genesis of a neurosis or psychosis – and thus to attribute them new meaning, can modify their negative effects. Precisely such events – which in ideal situations we sometimes regard as accidental and avoidable – need to be reconsidered, and viewed as parts of the process of the realization of an individual existence. It then grows clear that the suffering involved in such events is itself a necessary part of the generation of present and future psychological processes.

Various psychodynamic models have demonstrated how the psychological development of the child unfolds as a third solution to the tension between opposing polarities (gratification and frustration, fascination with the past and the drive toward the future, etc.), and have further shown such tensions to be necessary for the production of developmental energy. The child begins at birth to articulate its own development by growing accustomed to the "suffering" that derives from the loss and abandonment of a constant bond with the parent figures, and later from having to learn to postpone or relinquish the satisfaction of primitive needs and desires – and as well to abandon idealizations – as a basic condition for the pleasurable enjoyment of what life has to offer.

When such a renunciation takes place within the therapeutic process, patients can grow aware of the fragility of their parents. They can understand that their parents too were unable to behave differently, since they too are victims who have had no other model than what they learned from own families of origin, in what is usually a chain of unconscious suffering, both endured and imposed.

If acknowledgement of trauma and deficiencies, and of the feelings and emotions that go along with them, opens up possible routes of awareness that interrupt the blind repetition of suffering from one generation to the next, the constellation of the Self and a different activation of the archetypes can correct developmental distortions. In addition, the constellation of the Self and the family archetype, within the therapeutic relationship, activates self-healing and aspects of transformation that modify the image which the individual has of him- or herself and which is active in the world, as much as the family model that orients and structures both inner and outer relations. Such a re-elaboration of family roots can provide a patient – no matter if a child, an adolescent or an adult – with a new model of family realization. "Destiny" ceases to be a mere repetition of trauma, and instead becomes the realization of inborn potential, and of a unique and authentic individuality.

References

Baldassare, S., Bufacchi, C. (2001), *"Prospettive future: più spazio al tre o uno ripetuto infinite volte?,"* in *Studi Junghiani,* 13.

Bernhard, E. (1969), *Mitobiografia*, Adelphi, Milano.

Bick, E. (1964), "Notes on Infant Observation in Psycho-Analytic Training," in *International Journal of Psycho-Analysis*, 45.

Ellenberger H.F. (1970), *The Discovery of Unconscious. The History and Evolution of Dynamic Psychiatry*, Basic Books, New York.

Fivaz-Depeursinge, E., Corboz-Warnery, A.(1999), *The Primary Triangle*, Basic Books, New York.

Fordham, M. (1944-1969), *Children as Individuals,* Putnam, New York, 1972.

Franz, von, M.L. (1964), "The Process of Individuation," in C.G. Jung (Editor), *Man and His Symbols*, Aldus Books, London.

Jung, C.G. (1909-1949), "The Significance of the Father in the Destiny of the Individual," in *Collected Works*, vol. 4, Princeton University Press, Princeton, 1961.

Jung, C. G. (1910-1946), "Psychic Conflicts in a Child," in *Collected Works*, vol. 17, Princeton University Press, Princeton, 1954.

Jung, C. G. (1912-1952), *Symbols of Transformation,* in *Collected Works*, vol. 5, Princeton University Press, Princeton, 1956.

Jung, C. G. (1913), "The Theory of Psychoanalysis," in *Collected Works*, vol. 4, Princeton University Press, Princeton, 1961.

Jung, C. G. (1916-1948), "General Aspects of Dream Psychology," in *Collected Works*, vol. 8, Princeton University Press, Princeton, 1960.

Jung, C. G. (1928a), "The Relations between the Ego and the Unconscious," in *Collected Works*, vol. 7, Princeton University Press, Princeton, 1953.

Jung, C. G. (1928b), "On Psychic Energy," in *Collected Works*, vol. 8, Princeton University Press, Princeton, 1960.

Jung, C.G. (1928-1931), "Analytical Psychology and *Weltanschauung*," in *Collected Works*, vol. 8, Princeton University Press, Princeton, 1960.

Jung, C.G. (1935-1954), "The Archetypes of the Collective Unconscious," in *Collected Works*, vol. 9, part I, Princeton University Press, Princeton, 1959.

Jung, C.G. (1939-1954), "Psychological Aspects of the Mother Archetype," in *Collected Works*, vol. 9, part I, Princeton University Press, Princeton, 1959.

Jung, C.G. (1944), *Psychology and Alchemy, Collected Works*, vol. 12, Princeton University Press, Princeton, 1953.

Jung, C.G. (1942-1948), "A Psychological Approach to the Dogma of the Trinity," in *Collected Works*, vol. 11, Princeton University Press, Princeton, 1958.

Jung, C.G. (1946), "The Psychology of the Transference," *Collected Works*, vol. 16, Princeton University Press, Princeton, 1966.

Jung, C.G. (1946-1948), "The Phenomenology of the Spirit in Fairytales," in *Collected Works*, vol. 9, part I, Princeton University Press, Princeton, 1959.

Jung, C.G. (1951), *Aion, Collected Works*, vol. 9, part 2, Pantheon Books, Princeton, New York, 1959.

Kalff, D.M. (1966), *Sandplay: A Psychoterapeutic Approach to the Psyche*, Los Angeles, Sigo Press, 1981.

Kalsched (1996), *The Inner World of Trauma. Archetypical Defence of the Personal Spirit,* Routledge, London, New York.

Montecchi, F. (1989), "Child abuse e sand play therapy," in *Rivista di psicologia analitica*, 39.

Montecchi, F. (1993*), Giocando con la sabbia. La psicoterapia con bambini e adolescenti e la "sand play therapy,"* Franco Angeli, Milano.

Montecchi, F. (1995), "Il processo di individuazione nelle fasi dello sviluppo infantile," in *I simboli dell'infanzia. Dal pensiero di Jung al lavoro clinico con i bambini*, Carocci, Roma, 1998.

Montecchi, F. (1997a), "Famiglia reale e archetipo familiare," in F. Montecchi (a cura di), *Il gioco della sabbia nella pratica analitica*, Franco Angeli, Milano.

Montecchi, F. (1997b), "Le mani che parlano e l'ascolto analitico," in F. Montecchi (a cura di), *Il gioco della sabbia nella pratica analitica*, Franco Angeli, Milano.

Neumann, E. (1949), *The Origins and History of Consciousness,* Princeton University Press, Princeton, 1954.

Neumann, E. (1963), *The Child. Structure and Dynamics of the Nascent Personality,* Putnam's Sons, New York, 1973.

Schillirò, C. (2000), *Immagini del Sé positivo e del Sé negativo nell'arte e nella terapia,* in Associazione Italiana di Psicologia Analitica A.I.P.A., *Il Sé nella Teoria e nella Clinica.* AIPA, Roma.

Sidoli, M. (1989), *The Unfolding Self. Separation and Individuation,* Sigo Press, Boston.

Stern, D.N. (1985), *The Interpersonal World of the Infant,* Basic Books, New York.

Stern, D.N. (1995), *The Motherhood Constellation. A Unified View of Parent-Infant Psychotherapy,* Basic Books, New York.

Winnicott, D.W. (1960), "Ego Distortion in Terms of the True and False Self," in *The Maturational Processes and the Facilitating Environment,* Hogarth Press, London.

Zoja, L. (1986), "Psicologia analitica e metapsicologia dei sentimenti. Possibile coerenza tra Jung e Melanie Klein," in L. Zoja (a cura di), *La psicologia analitica di fronte alle altre psicologie del profondo,* Bertani, Verona.

Zoja, L. (2001), *The Father, Historical, Psychological and Cultural Perspectives,* Routledge, London.

Image and the Analytical Relationship in Sandplay Therapy

Wilma Bosio

"First, she warns, we must steer clear of the sirens,
their enchanting song, their meadow strewed with flowers.
I alone was to hear their voices, she said,
but you must bind me with tight chafing ropes
so I cannot move a muscle, bound to the spot,
erect at the mast-block, lashed by ropes to the mast.
And if I plead, commanding you to set me free,
then lash me faster, rope on pressing rope."

Odyssey, Book XII, 172-179

More than twenty years ago, while still a young psychologist in training, I attended a congress, in Rome, of Jungian child psychologists from all parts of Europe. One of them was Dora Kalff.

She followed a speaker whose presentation of a clinical case had literally stunned his public, thanks to his over-interpretation of the behavior of his young patient.

Kalff was a liberation. As she spoke, I had the thought: "If my daughter should ever be in need of help, I'll take her to Dora Kalff."

The highly beautiful images she showed were surely a part of what I found so convincing, but I was first of all impressed by her attitude to the patients whose creations she presented. She communicated a great sense of calm and peace of mind, and I intuited her ability to help my interior daughter, who was still in difficulty.

Two years later I began my sessions in Zollikon, and later my training in sandplay therapy. I had been struck by the images and the therapist's attitude, and now I rediscovered them, along with the alliance and the challenge which they would then continue to offer in the further development of my profession as an analyst. The words Kalff spoke in the course of my personal experience with her continued to be rare and precious, just as at the time when I first encountered her.

The receptive but largely silent atmosphere in which they found their origin was amplified by the half darkness of the old house, immersed in turn in Zollikon's quiet.

Silence and interior listening are parts of every good therapy, and sandplay therapy views them as indispensable, at least in the first phase of the treatment, and especially with respect to its aspect of interpretation. In this sense, the attitude of the therapist who works with sandplay shows no great difference from the analyst's respect for the manifest content of dreams recounted in the course of a session, with its principle of avoiding foregone conclusions or reductive comments. Yet, a difference can be found insofar as this respect in sandplay is more total. It's as though the therapist's intervention doesn't limit itself to stimulating a dialog with the images by way of offering amplifications, and remains in suspension somewhat earlier, waiting for the image itself, in its real three-dimensionality, to lead the ego to a dialog.

Since its earliest years of application, and then of its diffusion in the world of Jungian analysis, sandplay has been met not only by benevolent and even enthusiastic receptions, but also by a certain diffidence. Certain sorts of prejudice tend to devalue it, and thus as well to restrict its field of application. Verbal language has always ranked as the vehicle and mediator of the analytical relationship, as the essential tool through which to decodify the transference and countertransference, and the fact that its use is here, in sandplay, seen to be of limited relevance has certainly helped to nourish an attitude of diffidence and devaluation. A therapy in which little is said risks being taken for a therapy in which one doesn't know what's taking place, or where little or nothing may in fact take place; or at least where what takes place encounters no consciousness that integrates it. Primary emphasis on the importance of sandplay images as such, without further reference to patients' conscious attitudes, may therefore have contributed to hasty devaluations. So, the best way to counter such impressions is by offering reflections which on the one hand take account of the image, while on the other doing justice to the conscious work of both patient and analyst.

The images exert a great fascination on those who observe them, and this is even more the case when the images hold archaic contents, or mainly give expression to materials from the collective unconscious. While drawing a distinction between primordial images and personal images, Jung considers the image to be connected only indirectly to the perception of external objects. In psychological terms, the image has the features of an imaginative representation; and this interior image is always distinct from sense perceptible reality: it's a concentrated expression of a total psychic situation, since it's an expression of the contents constellated in the moment in which it was formed.[1]

On the one hand, we're dealing with the powers of seduction exercised by the collective unconscious. And on the other, we're dealing with the ego, with the ego's historical past, and as well with its present circumstances, which also include its encounter with the analyst's personality. These are the contents of all analytical situations, with the difference that for sandplay, the encounter with the collective unconscious is activated at a somewhat earlier point than in the case of verbal analysis, thanks to its introduction of a confrontation with primordial images in analytical relationships that have only recently begun.

This is why our headquote refers to Ulysses, and to the subterfuge that allowed him to listen to the Sirens while preventing him from falling into their all-dissolving embrace. After his stay with Circe, the great enchantress who wields the power to transform men into animals, Ulysses must next resist the call of the Sirens. Circe had learned of Ulysses' arrival from an oracle, and recognized his superiority. She offered herself to him, and she freed his companions whom she had already turned into pigs. Circe is an anima figure, and Homer gave her the role of pointing out the route of the descent into Hades, and then of the dangers of the return.

So we have to be able to order ourselves to be tied to the mast of the ship, and to warn whoever assists us that we're not to be untied, since we understand the greatness of the power of the unconscious. Lashed to the mast, we have to resist all sorts of traps and seductions, which only an honest and constant confrontation with the shadow allows us to recognize. As circumstances vary, the companions on our voyage can offer help, or must be held at bay, or invite us to adhere more tenaciously to a therapy and a project. The myth also tells us, in metaphoric terms, that we must never forget our frailty and other shortcomings: instead we're to assume responsibility for them, making use of the instruments supplied by the analysis of the transference and the countertransference, and by a century of psychoanalytical history.

Jung wrote in 1928: "For two personalities to meet is like mixing two different chemical substances: if there is any combination at all, both are transformed. In any effective psychological treatment the doctor is bound to influence the patient; but this influence can only take place if the patient has a reciprocal influence on the doctor. You can exert no influence if you are not susceptible to influence. It is futile for the doctor to shield himself from the influence of the patient and to surround himself with a smoke-screen of fatherly and professional authority. By so doing he only denies himself the use of a highly important organ of information. The patient influences him unconsciously none the less, and brings about changes in the doctor's unconscious which are well known to many psychotherapists: psychic disturbances or even injuries peculiar to the profession, a striking illustration of the patient's almost 'chemical' action."[2]

So, psychic contagion makes the undertaking difficult, but is nonetheless an essential instrument for reaching a knowledge of the other.

Sandplay as the Method of Choice

Fordham's distinction, drawn in 1956, between "imaginative activity" and "active imagination"[3] strikes me as useful for a description of the states that normally succeed one another in a properly functioning sandplay process.

Patients at the start are often quite defensive, and belittle their constructions, or construct them with reference to the places or facts of their lives. The ego here is passive, and it's only with the passage of time that "active imagination" begins to make its appearance, with its implication of an ego that actively confronts imagination.

Experience reveals this shift to take place after a more or less extended process of playing, and its appearance, in any case, grows more distinct when the unconscious ceases primarily to show its negative aspect, and instead becomes the seat of a process of transformation; and as such it nurtures the deprived and needy ego to the point of leading it to a renewal that finds expression in the always moving rebirth images that by now have been discussed in any number of contributions to the sandplay literature. In more or less artistic ways, according to the patient's personality – but in ways which are always highly original – these cases show the paths of a process of individuation, and thereby reveal the method's extraordinary usefulness for a large number of neurotic patients. Sandplay therapy, in some of these cases, can even be seen as the "method of choice," in the sense that it gives the impression of being an approach that it would be difficult to replace with others, even if it's clear that there can be no proof of any such affirmation.

The therapist's silence during sandplay is always a silence which is highly receptive of everything that is taking place in the therapy room: tentative words and glances, repetitions, the tones of words and glances, along with the emotions, sensations and moments of discomfort that the situation may excite. All of this is then finally flanked by an image – either with or without objects – which constitutes something that the patient and the whole of the session can be said to have birthed: it results from an encounter between two different psychologies, even if they're greatly confused with one another, as especially in the treatment's opening phase.

In the fortunate cases where this temporary initial confusion in no way jeopardizes the treatment's continuation – and, indeed, it often bolsters it – one may also encounter an ever more conspicuous shift in the attitude which the patient shows to the images that he or she produces. This shift is also a demonstration of what at times is a radical change of consciousness, and of the patient's whole attitude to life. The characteristic one-sidedness of the initial phases of treatment is followed by the typical fluidity of the symbolic dimension that comes into play in individuals who are able to move into "the third area," to used Winnicott's well-known phrase: the "as if" area where it is possible to relate to realities that are not concrete as outwardly observable phenomena.

The passage to the symbolic dimension is often announced by the use of figures that speak of mysterious things, which, like angels, can communicate with extra-worldly dimensions; or there may be animals that can see in the dark; or wise men or seers who point out occult paths; or fantasy figures that converse with dangerous beasts that others are unable to see. These figures attest to the patient's having made a connection with the archetypal world that presents itself as the source of hope, rebirth, and transformation.

The verbal language that accompanies the construction of the image characterizes the patient's attitude to his or her creations. And the patient's conscious attitude, as Jung has told us, reflects the power of the patient's resistances, and as such can help us evaluate the level of enmity between the two opposing systems. The attitude shown to the initial sand constructions will in fact be partial and reductive in direct proportion to the degree of dissociation from which the patient suffers, and the therapist's task is therefore to take custody of the symbolic meaning of the figures and the overall scene, so as to compensate the dissociation which works within the patient, and which holds the patient in alienation from him- or herself. In this sense, the therapist serves as precursor and mediator of the transcendent function, which is the source of what Jung identifies as the very goal of therapy. That goal is to produce a psychic state in which the patient begins to experience his or her nature as existing in a state of fluidity, change, and becoming, where nothing is eternally fixed, petrified, or hopeless.

Two sand pictures constructed by a patient in the course of a three-year analysis (two pictures from a total of thirty-five pictures) can exemplify this change of attitude with respect to one's psychic world.

Maria was thirty years old, and presented symptoms of hysteria, including an intermittent paralysis of her right hand, a condition which created considerable problems in her work as a secretary. She still lived with her parents, but had a highly ambivalent relationship with them, and for the past several years she had accepted the attentions of a married man who showered her with gifts, but who had no intention of leaving his wife for her.

Maria was entirely at the service of her family and her lover, and constantly complained about everything, tearing herself apart but putting up with it all, and her illness lay in her inability to reach decisions or to assume responsibility for her own life.

Without entering into particulars, we could say that something had been missing from her childhood and adolescence, causing her to distance from herself, and paralyzing her ability to adapt to reality. This, in turn, explains the reason for her libido's having been introverted, with the result that the patient lived in a world that belonged to her childhood, and lost herself in difficulties that seemed to lie outside of time. Her ego had lost its connections with instinct and had atrophied; she seemed destined to remain unconscious of herself and dependent on her parents. She could no longer stand them, but she couldn't separate from them, since that would kill them.

Like all hysterics, she felt a great desire for access to a spiritual dimension, but without being able to achieve it. She suffered from an interior blockage that prevented her from opening up to the realm of symbol, and which threw its energy back into the body, or into a symptom of somatic conversion.

Figure 1

In the first sandplay construction – made after seven months of twice weekly therapy, characterized overall by wails and lamentations, also of course about the therapist – we see the sandbox unequally divided by a stream just barely hinted at.

The stream of water holds apart a series of representations of gods that the patient does not know, and behind them stands a princess, as well as a sacrificed sheep on an altar on the right side. In this larger part, we see a small, lifeless village, constructed at the side of the river, and a somewhat saccharine scene with a monk who is waiting at the door of the church for a group of simple people on Christmas eve. Among them is a small, sleeping boy.

In the course of her associations, Maria referred to the oriental gods as "black shadows," and related that they hold the princess prisoner. And the princess, in turn, feels herself to be a sacrificial victim, clearly alluding to the lamb on the altar, whereas what she wants is to live the happy, carefree life she had known as a child during Christmas vacations. The monk reminded her of her childhood parish priest, and she said that his path to his vows had been charged with great suffering.

This first sand construction offers an overview of the entirety of the patient's psychic situation, while also exhibiting elements of transformation.

We can say that the patient's ego would like to lead a life that's free from conflicts and problems, whereas in fact she sees herself as a sacrificial victim, immolated in the name of a meaningless life. She's trapped in the image of a rigid princess, and detached from reality. She feels herself to be a victim, yet does not know that the only way to give her existence dignity would lie in the sacrifice of her links with her childhood and her parents, who are deformed by her own projections. But to do such a thing would demand a faith in a spiritual potential which as yet she doesn't possess. Yet, the infantile dream in which she's imprisoned also contains the germs of a transformation: in the sleeping child and the priest whose past was full of suffering. Sandplay gave this young woman a way to set out on an imaginative voyage that led to an encounter with a pair of wolves that seemed finally to offer her companionship throughout the whole of a series of adventures and fantastic struggles. These adventures, however, ever more clearly revealed themselves to be a true and proper initiation into the difficulties of life; and in the course of this initiation, passive attitudes were progressively abandoned, and made ever more room for the patient's growing faith in her own abilities, and in her power to listen to herself.

Figure 2

This second sand construction, a year later than the first, and from just about the middle of the patient's analysis, reveals her shift of attitude to internal and outer reality: seeing herself as a victim had kept her alienated from life, and now she's on her way to overcoming that point of view.

The scene shows a "squaw" who lives "by choice" in a small village, and takes care of a two year old boy. Nearby are a number of very special blue horses, "which allow her to escape whenever she wants to" and a black man who carries a quantity of appetizing fruits. These fruits, however, are something extra, and at the moment "one can also do without them."

This scene is a part of a moment with continuing connotations of depression, but it's also marked by a totally new tone and quality of feeling, as compared to those of the initial phase of therapy.

There's an interior world which is not unendurable, for which one has opted by choice, and from which it is also possible temporarily to take one's distance; and more than anything else, there's a return to a simpler and more instinctive way of life that also holds implications of a practicable self-sufficiency. The princess who before was the victim of an intolerable situation has here been replaced by the squaw: the image of a simple femininity, in harmony with the instincts, from which the patient can again start out to find a space of her own in the world, in accordance with her talents and potential. This change of perspective revealed itself within the transference as an abandonment of attitudes of vindictiveness and victimization; and in the external world it corresponded to the assumption of commitments consonant with the patient's abilities, and to a great increase of self-sufficiency in the wake of her abandoning her relationship with the man who had never made a true commitment to her. He had represented an immature form of masculinity, charged with illusions, and had never been capable of putting up any kind of fight or making any sort of sacrifice for her.

I don't want to go too far into this particular case, which, like many others, has interesting facets. It does, however, make it possible to raise the question of the specificity of sandplay therapy.

With a case of such a nature, it seems unlikely that exclusive use of verbal analysis could have led to a radical change in the patient's situation in a reasonably limited period of time; we're dealing here with a patient who communicated very little, cried a great deal, didn't remember her dreams, and apparently derived scant benefit from analytical work on the transference. With this particular patient, as in other similar cases, sandplay therapy revealed itself to be truly the method of choice, and considerably effective, even on the longer term. It is a question of cases where the transference not only involves the projection of infantile conflicts onto the therapist, but also activates a process of individuation which pushes the patient not only to discover his or her identity and to function better in the world, but also to improve their relationship with potentials that aren't the simple privilege of any individual, and in fact belong to all.

The common denominator of the cases that overcome neurotic splits and where the patients change their attitude towards both themselves and life as a whole can be found in the fact that the patient experienced damage to the ability to elaborate symbol at a time when the basis for such operations had already been laid in the mother-child relationship, but then suffered a blockage that prevented their maturation. The process of growth and evolution has been arrested for these sorts of patients, but they discover the warmth of the analytical situation to furnish a condition that permits resumption of their interrupted development.

Countertransference and Sandplay in Difficult Cases

We have nonetheless observed that the perception of sandplay as a free and protected space is a difficult point of arrival for certain patients to achieve. The dilemmas they have to overcome are so extreme as to make it impossible. The reference here is to cases where the relationship between patient and therapist is characterized by a prevalence of acting out, and where the mechanism primarily at work is projective identification. These are cases in which sandplay will very probably be rejected, since it's highly difficult to establish a relation of basic trust between the patient and the therapist.

We have also noted that when sandplay is used on a highly sporadic basis, without ever being seen, even for a limited period of time, as what we've called the "method of choice," it seems to take on functions which are largely a question of communications inside the analytical relationship. There's an apparent desire to please the therapist, but it frequently as well conceals the possibility of giving the therapist an indication that a moment is particularly difficult. That information can be effectively hidden in images that apparently (for the patient) hold no meaning.

Sandplay, even in a mode of minimum participation, demands a loss of control; and loss of control is something which these sorts of patients cannot tolerate, not even to a minor degree.

The experience of the countertransference is greatly marked by feelings of suffocation, impotence, and constriction; and this can lead to collusion with the patient's rigidity, as expressed at times through requests, at others through acts of rejection. So a suggestion on the part of the therapist to work with sandplay can amount to a route of escape for both; and instead of creating a free and protected space, the game reproduces the same vindictive, angry space in which the patient is already trapped, and which cannot lead to any transformation.

The purpose of sandplay is to soften the patient's defenses, but its use becomes fruitless and pointless in all those cases where the patient's defenses are flanked by those of the analyst. The analyst, in such situations, becomes collusive, and can therefore do no proper analytical work, at least until such time and he/she doesn't grow conscious of what is taking place. The analyst's vision, in cases like these, is clouded; and at times, even while perceiving that the moment is charged with difficulties, the analyst may tend to minimize them. The analyst becomes distracted from a proper analysis of the countertransference, and instead becomes caught up in the objective problems that exert their weight on the patient, and which finally end up by corrupting the analyst's perceptions as well. This a kind of situation that prevents the analyst from attempting to clarify the nature of his or her feelings, or from seeing if they have to be attributed to the analyst's own complexes, or to the patient's projections.

I can give the example of the case of a nearly sixty year old woman who after ten months of therapy encountered a difficult passage and interrupted her analysis. The sand construction to which I refer was created eight months after the beginning of treatment.

Lucia was the mother of three children and had been married for more than thirty years to a man who was highly cultivated, but seriously disturbed. After ten years of marriage, his borderline personality had revealed itself through a series of explosions of unspeakable violence against objects and his wife. The explosions came always in the wake of apparently insignificant arguments which, in any case, were always related to discussions of cultural questions: discussions which the woman attempted in vain to avoid, since she was always the loser, and finally silenced or ridiculed.

The first months of therapy had been characterized by an extremely spectacular account of her life as a girl, told as though recounting a novel. The presentation was rich with melodramatic details that also tended to be somewhat seductive. The patient had reached the point at which the relative security she was little by little acquiring had exacerbated her internal conflicts: on the one hand stood the possibility of reacquiring significance within her marriage, of making real decisions about her life and the use of her time, and even perhaps of leaving her husband; on the other hand stood the danger of giving in to her fear of her husband, and of continuing to accept his violent and sadistic abuses.

Figure 3

The image shows a small lake with a number of boats, on one of which a fisherman is attempting to land "a precious fish," while not too far away is a shark that intends to take it away from him. Lower down, there's a small boy in the water, next to a naked woman who's lying in the sun, and who seems to pay no attention to him. The patient remarks, "Maybe the shark will win the battle."

The image constructed in the sand reveals the conflict between her desire to capture something of value, and her unconscious resistance to any such undertaking, as expressed by the shark.

We must also add that the patient's inner maternal attitude was insufficiently developed: it's apparently trapped in narcissism (the woman sunbathes naked, but pays no attention to her child). This was further confirmed by an association with her youngest daughter, who was highly beautiful, quite precocious and much "adored," but not really seen or adequately taken care of.

The thought of taking herself seriously – her life, her tastes, her potential – was the source of an intolerable conflict with her family situation, since at this particular moment the patient equated any such action with leaving her husband, and thus to killing him or being killed. So, it seemed to her that her only possible course of action was to leave things just as they had stood before this conflict had reached its present level of intensity. This also meant that she'd have to interrupt her analysis, which was responsible at least for a sharpening of the conflict.

The patient's sand construction can indeed be seen to have furnished a negative prediction on the conflict's further development, but the therapist didn't take her seriously enough. Lack of comprehension of the state of affairs then repeated itself in the following sessions: the patient began to arrive late, and the therapist showed no appropriate recognition of the reasons for the patient's tardiness. The sessions became the scene of a diabolic repetition of the situation at the patient's home, where there was never a chance for what she thought to be given consideration, since she was "ignorant and stupid and thoroughly incapable of thinking with her own head."

The analyst, in fact, had been mesmerized by the patient's reports on her husband's violence, which seemed to have increased, as indeed was quite probable, in the light of the patient's achievement of a less passive attitude. The analyst shared the patient's perplexities on what to do, and meanwhile never managed to think back to the reasons for the patient's tardiness. The analyst's behavior was much like the patient's, who acted out her problem, by way of tardiness, without being able to talk about it.

The patient's repeated lateness was probably an expression of a slow but inexorable retreat from the acts of self-reflection which the woman had begun to undertake in the course of her analysis. Or she might be said to have wanted to diminish the scope of any such reflections. At the very same time, she was also reaching a highly delicate juncture at which the conflict between the ego and the Self was growing more exasperated, and all in the absence of a sufficiently supportive bond between patient and analyst.

The sand construction and the tardiness signaled an arrest of confidence, as well as fear, but weren't given sufficient consideration. The patient's sense of abandonment was thus confirmed, since psychological abandonment is precisely what the therapist was acting out by showing herself incapable of properly thinking about her patient.

Here, as in all difficult cases, the analysis of the counter-transference reveals itself to be an indispensable tool, on a par with the patient's images and words, for tearing away the direction of the analytical process from the unconscious, and in this case from the Uroboric unconscious, which is the enemy of transformation. The analyst allowed herself to be distracted by the problem of what to do about the patient's husband – a problem with apparently no solution – and meanwhile repressed perception of the upsurge of self-deprecation that the patient was currently experiencing, as expressed at this point by her tardiness, and by her laments about her husband.

The therapist had felt that they were passing through a difficult moment and had therefore proposed a sandplay session. The patient had accepted the suggestion with a derisive and deprecatory attitude, which with hindsight reveals how her defenses were in fact at the service of the Uroboric unconscious, as a force of involution and negativity.

The analyst and the patient acted in ways that compensated for one another: the patient's radical lack of confidence was countered by the analyst's excessive confidence. This means, in turn, that the analyst was incapable of remaining inside the conflict, and fled from it just as the patient was doing.

Lucia's comment on the image – a comment she made without awareness of its reference to an intrapsychic content ("maybe the shark will win the battle") signaled the presence of an overbearing unconscious by which the still weak ego, without the benefit of spiritual allies, can only be devoured.

This case exemplifies the fact that sandplay is an integral part of the therapeutic process, and can be never be separated from it. It's a part of a relationship in which the vigilance of the therapist – despite the inevitability of reciprocal confusion – must always be maintained.

Anna

In other cases, the minimum feeling of basic trust which is indispensable for sandplay can require long periods of preparation. These are cases where the patient's primary relationship with his or her parents has been so dramatically damaged as to demand that patient and therapist experience a lengthy acquaintanceship before reaching a renewed experience of basic trust and confidence from which to redepart, and through which as well to hold psychic monsters at bay. These are cases where the use of sandplay is an important point of arrival: a rediscovery of the possibility not only of play, but of life. And it comes in the wake of a lengthy mothering process which has managed to recreate a fundamental sense of security.

I think back, for example, to Anna, who had decided to begin an analytical therapy after years of desperation in which she had thought quite often, and seriously, about suicide. That was a point, in any case, which she seemed slowly to be reaching, given her total lack of all vitality or enthusiasm. She ate very little, and survived "in spite of herself" in a situation which she experienced as intolerable and highly painful, both at home, where she continued to live which her parents, and at work, for a social agency.

Anna had been five years old when her mother had been hospitalized for seven months in a sanatorium for pulmonary tuberculosis. Both of her parents were aged, very industrious workers, and very stiff. At the time of her conception, Anna's father was sixty-five, and her mother was forty-five.

Anna had continued to live with her father and had only once been able to visit her mother during the period of her illness, and when that had taken place she had touched her only with a finger, without being able to hug her, since she was just that paralyzed by the certainty that the woman before her was dead. And shortly afterward, she began to be plagued by a terrible anxiety which, later, when she was larger, she had baptized "the thing." "The thing" almost never abandoned her, with the exception of when she studied, repeating her lessons by rote, like a parrot: she managed to fill up the space of her anxiety with a kind of singsong, and thus to hold the monster at bay.

"The thing" found its origins in acts of betrayal on the part of both her parents: one of them had fallen ill, and the other had begun to surround her with morbid attentions and caresses that culminated in half hidden acts of masturbation which the little girl was forced to watch, on a variety of makeshift pretexts.

The father's horrid, underhanded behavior then continued after Anna's mother returned, up until Anna's adolescence, when she began more effectively to defend herself, no longer responding when her father summoned her, or treating him badly on other occasions, yet never finding the courage to mention to anyone what she had been subjected to. At the time she entered therapy, Anna was thirty years old, but looked as though she were twelve. And in addition to being extremely thin and speaking with a little girl's voice, she emitted a strange, unpleasant odor, as skunks do, to hold others at a distance.

After a year and a half of analysis, Anna – who had always passed through the sandplay room nearly at a run, without ever stopping – asked if her sessions might be held there, only to be able to see the toys and figures from a distance. Later, however, she began to hold a doll in her arms and would cradle it throughout her sessions, caressing it and beginning a mothering process which involved me too in caring for it.

From this moment on, the sandplay room was never again abandoned: it became the appointed place for a long, mutual effort of custody. The doll had to be fed and allowed to grow up in a place that was full of warmth, free of ambiguities and blackmail: a place that allowed the intensely painful re-emergence of memories – memories which were also quite precious – of suffering, privation, and psychological abandonment. Actual, physical care for this figure continued until the patient was attracted by another doll that represented a pre-school age girl who was dressed in a way quite similar to her own at the time when her life had gone to pieces, after separation from her mother.

A new game began with this second doll. Anna made it walk along the edges of the sandbox, then she dared to take a step or two inside it, and at the end of the session she placed it inside the sandbox, along with a fire and a supply of food. This was nearly as though she were reconfirming her ability to pass into another dimension for which she had made her preparations by taking care of the first doll. The patient then continued to work with sand, mainly without accompanying objects, and she progressively acquired, session after session, a diminishing control of her communications. Anna had always communicated her memories, her dreams, and the salient events of her daily life with a certain delay; she didn't report them in the moment in which they came to mind, and it was rather as though she felt the need to subject her emotional life to a kind of obsessive, apotropaic control in order to strip it of anything dangerous.

The therapy entered an important crisis after the fifth year, when control of the situation was lessening, and the patient's dependence on the therapist had grown deeper and therefore more dangerous. She frequently called the office answering machine to hear the therapist's voice, or to make certain that the therapist was still alive, since she feared that she might devour her, as a result of her "extreme" need of the therapist's physical presence. The transference led her back through the critical point of the trauma she had undergone, and then she was able with the following representation in sand to give symbolic expression to the possibility of containing and being contained.

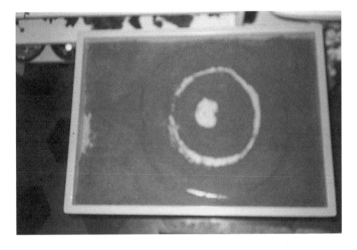

Figure 4

This construction shows a central hole, surrounded by a circle and the traces left by the hands of the patient and the analyst, the one right next to the other, on the left-hand side of the sandbox, "to hold the hole together, the thing." Then the hands were represented with molding clay, starting again from an impression of her own hand and the analyst's, this time, however, in direct and more intentional contact.

Figure 5

In the following construction, a few sessions later, she was able to represent a small village, with a tower from which dinosaurs could be seen in the distance. By now, however, they were held in isolation on an island, kept separate from the village by a huge bridge, all covered with vegetation, which traversed the sandbox up to the top of its outside edge.

Figure 6

The therapeutic alliance permitted her to control from a distance the pathogenic complex, as expressed by the island inhabited by dinosaurs, and it also allowed her to communicate with the outside world, thus expressing her ability to make the distinction between inside and outside, to tolerate separation, and to deal with the mourning it caused.

After this construction, the patient felt a great deal better psychologically, but began to grow physically ill, which was quite atypical, since she had never given signs of physical weakness. She caught a bad influenza, then an ear infection, then scarlet fever: she was finally becoming normal.

Her libido seemed to have come unblocked, and shortly later – as I continue to find incredible – she met a man who was somewhat older than herself, but very timid and clumsy. He was a person with whom this still frozen woman could find the warmth that allowed her to express herself, thus also helping the analysis to reach its conclusion. For another two years she elaborated her differentiation from her mother who, having remained a widow, always encircled her with tremendous acts of blackmail.

At a later point, during a visit to the therapist, after the completion of the restoration of the church at Assisi, where the frescos had been nearly pulverized by an earthquake, she remarked, "You know, doctor, when I saw the pictures of that disaster I thought that it would have been impossible to do anything about it, exactly the way I felt when I first came to see you: I felt like something that nothing could be done about."

This very moving case – like all the more difficult cases – in which sandplay was employed, but in a very limited and accessory way, owes its happy conclusion to the reconstruction of a fundamental trust, and thus to the creation of a relationship that was capable of holding monsters at bay.

For this patient, playing with the doll, in an experience lived out directly with the therapist, signaled the need entirely to re-travel her path of differentiation, starting from the very beginning. The therapist was initially asked to take part in a fairly passive way, in the role of protector, and at times as consultant, and the goal was for the patient to reappropriate her ability to be a child in the company of her mother, safe from the intrusion of every form of violation, which in her own historical past had taken the form of her mother's illness and her father's sexual perversion.

It's as though the process of identification had in this case been so damaged as to demand a reconstruction from the beginning, a restoration that nearly amounted to a whole new act of creation, as in the restoration of the church at Assisi, to which the patient referred during her visit. In order to achieve her differentiation, she had to relearn the experience of being a child; and through the symbiotic situation which she shared with her therapist, she was able to do so from the very start, from the moment of nursing.

The patient's access to the sphere of symbol would seem in this case to have been blocked by a traumatic situation which fortunately had not been too precocious, but which still had been so violent as profoundly to compromise her possibility of leading an existence even at a very elementary level. "The return to the mothers," through suicide, had seemed to be the only possible exit strategy from an intolerable conflict. Her life had been a living hell; she felt safe and redeemed only in the therapy room.

It was Anna who had directed a play situation that the therapist then accepted, permitting her to reappropriate the ability to take care of herself, in a protected situation where it was possible to express a need that would otherwise have been difficult to integrate. Anna offers a radical example of the need to recuperate an identity situation that prepares an awareness of bonds and differentiations; and she reached that awareness at the moment of the therapy's crisis, which then she was able to overcome by expressing herself in sandplay constructions; and the possibility of sandplay had in turn been due to what her work with her therapist already had allowed her to re-experience.

In some way, Anna refers us back to a primary phase: to the identity situation of fullness and protection and containment within the Self of the mother. Her process of acting out in the analytical situation – and she acted out a vital necessity – is in some ways comparable to the requests for elaboration and emotional rumination which patients who suffer from affects that cannot be elaborated entrust to or thrust upon the analyst. But here the situation is also different, insofar as it foresees a simpler solution of the disturbance, by way of a comprehensive re-elaboration of the whole course of the trauma.

There are other situations in which it's more difficult to recuperate conditions of fundamental trust, since to do so requires the recovery and translation into words of something that lies in a psychoid state, which in addition to emotional is also somatic. The patient, nonetheless, may be able to integrate such contents, or they may be able to serve as a bridge for an image – as in the case recounted by Eva Pattis elsewhere in this book – and thus open the road for other images.

In Anna's case, the mothering process which was carried out with the assistance of the therapist repaired the damage provoked by the trauma, and it did so by leading the patient backwards to an even anterior situation which perhaps already had laid the basis for the intensity of the pain that the subsequent trauma would cause.

This case also allows us a series of reflections on the consequences that this sort of primary relationship can bear for the formation of the animus in women. Anna's way of thinking was parrot-like and repetitive, or merely a question of filling up spaces. And confined as it was to an area of meaningless compulsion, it could lead to nothing original or creative. But little by little as the dyadic relation came to be repaired, Anna also experienced a loosening of control over the course of her thinking, which thus reacquired fluidity, naturalness, and even originality: her newly found access to the dimension of symbol came to be reflected in her thinking.

Conclusions

While accepting that Dora Kalff's vision of sandplay is based on the creation of a free and protected space, we'd assert that this condition can by no means be taken for granted: it's a highly fortunate condition, or at times can only be reached at the cost of a quantity of humble, attentive work which the analyst has to perform on the countertransference.

Such a free and protected space is often a difficult conquest, since the wounds which the patients have suffered in the primary relationship can go so deep as to demand that a great deal of work be done on the analytical relationship, as a prelude to achieving the requisite condition of a measure of basic trust.

To describe the analytical space as free and protected is to allude to a space where the analyst's Self and ego contain, assist, and render possible a process of repairing inadequate or insufficient relationships between the patients and their real parents. It's precisely because of their insufficiency that these relationships have non-voluntarily contributed to a condition of dependence on the part of a son or a daughter, and thus to a blockage of their differentiation and psychological growth. And what we finally have in this situation is a non-collusive analytical relationship between the analyst and a patient whose level of individuation has been held back.

In the case of the patient who serves as our first example, we are faced with an arrest of development accompanied by symptoms of hysteria. And after an initial few months of therapy, the patient rediscovered a sufficiently reassuring situation to be able by way of sandplay to find a route of approach to her distant, alienated interior.

In cases like these, the analyst is able to comprehend the symbolic value of the image the patient has constructed, and holds it in reserves in his/her own interior, trusting that the image itself will be able to activate and further a process that finds the therapist's warmth, attention and non-invasiveness to offer the fundamental alliance required for an effective transformation.

This is what we've used – in a very synthetic way, which is to say with the help of only two images, one initial and the other from what we've seen as a turning point in the process – to exemplify a patient's shift of attitude with respect to an inner conflict. And the shift is concerned not only with the images but also with accompanying associations, with the attitude in analysis, and also with the attitude to life in general, all of which appear to have undergone a change. A comparison of the two constructions reveals the elements of the first to present them-selves anew, but in terms of a reversal of their meaning. This amounts to an expression of a renewal of the ego, and speaks likewise of its relationship with the patient's more profound resources. The patient's task will be further to strengthen herself, and to make further use of the new resources now at her disposal. She'll continue for all the time that's needed for the creation of a state of personal autonomy.

The princess held trapped by black shadows had felt herself to be a sacrificial victim; but in the second construction she presents herself as a young squaw who chooses to live in her tribal camp and to attend to the needs of her baby. This is to be seen as a harbinger of a less conflictual and more natural attitude to inner and exterior reality. The renewed ego is no longer the slave of an unreachable ideal ego that lacks all vital relationship with the shadow. The scene we see in the Indian camp expresses this ego's ability to face the challenges of daily life, and to find no reason to feel entrapped by it.

We must also, however, remember that it isn't always possible to witness a profound renewal of the personality. This is partly due to the analyst's problems with this or that particular patient, and partly because certain patients have difficulties which are greater than those of the patient we have here discussed. There are difficult cases where differentiation is experienced as highly dangerous and destructive, and the use of sand isn't in itself a source of protection from the possibility of failure. We have come to feel that the therapeutic efficacy of sandplay can only be seen in the cases where analyst and patient have recreated a condition of basic trust. Such a condition is indispensable if the unconscious – which in this case loses its paralyzing quality – is to be allowed to direct the process of renewal.

G. Maffei has written, "In the area of transition, the psychic experience of a possibility of reciprocal transformation finds its source in the mother-child relationship, and then extends into outside reality: outside reality, just like the mother, can modify the child, and the child is likewise empowered to modify outside reality.... Once established in childhood, there's no natural way in which this belief can be uprooted: if the hope of altering reality and of making it accord with one's own desires has been established in childhood, then later, even in traumatic situations, it won't be able to disappear.... Everything that happens in the area of transition can be touched by a sense of life, and all the products of our psyche can be perceived as a gift to those around us. What the child has experienced as a passive state of harmony, tends to become an active one...."[4]

We'd add that this is exactly what one finds when sandplay is the method of choice, or the method seen as fundamental for any given patient. These are cases where the primary relationship was sufficiently good, and where the damage which the patient suffered didn't strike all the way down to the patient's very foundations. There are other cases in which these foundations have to be repaired, and if the attempt to repair them is not made, it is fairly likely that therapy will encounter failure.

Lucia's case – the case of the woman with the borderline husband – is an example of a therapy that didn't at first appear to be difficult, thanks to the seductive defenses that the patient called into play at the very start. But as things turned out, it finally revealed the precarious terrain on which it in fact had proceeded: a terrain where the conflict between a process of individuation and the resistance the patient deployed against it could find no symbolic resolution. Instead, it found expression in the patient's decision to interrupt the analytical relationship, and thus in a continuing condition of neurotic and non-evolving compulsion.

The third case again advises us of the real need for a fundamental relationship. It hinged on an actual, factual revisitation of the acts of maternal care, and the patient thus proved capable of rediscovering the emotional and spiritual resources through which to hold her personal monsters at bay: her monsters, her anxiety, her fear of annihilation.

In this last case, the sandplay room and its explicit allusion to the whole notion of play seems to have taken on the functions of a kind of cradle, awaiting a newborn child. It nurtured the patient's profound need for an experience of regression, and it was nearly as though contact with a space designed for play, and thus for psychological birth, was no less crucial than the carnal presence of the analyst/mother for the reactivation of the archetypal process which would once again connect her to life and its possible relationships.

References

1 Jung, C. G. (1971), *Psychological Types*, chapter XI, "Definitions," CW vol. 6, Princeton: Princeton University Press, pp. 442 – 447.
2 Jung, C.G. (1954/1966), *The Practice of Psychotherapy*, chapter V, "Problems of Modern Psychotherapy," CW vol. 16, Princeton: Princeton University Press, p. 71.
3 Fordham, M. (1956), "Active Imagination and Imaginative Activity," *Journal of Analytical Psychology*, Vol. I.
4 Maffei, G. (2000), *Le metafore*, Milan: Vivarium, p. 340.

Sacrifice as Death and Rebirth in Adolescent Development

Hypotheses on the genesis of the psychotic dynamic and its treatment: The case of a patient with a diagnosis of schizophrenia treated with sandplay therapy.

Lorenzo Bignamini

Jung was interested in adolescent mind states, such as those which could be observed in adult patients in which an active constellation of bursts of positivity and creativity exist alongside those of negativity and destruction.

Regarding adolescence as a developmental phase, Jung (1930) writes: "Psychic birth, and with it the conscious differentiation from the parents, normally takes place only at puberty, with the eruption of sexuality." (CW 8, paragraph 756, p. 391). The essay "Psychoanalytic Theory" (1913) responds to Freud's ideas about infantile sexuality, and Jung comments "Sexuality has an increasingly small share in pleasure-sensations the further back we go in childhood.... Certainly it is reinforced by a budding eroticism relatively early. This element gains strength as the years go on, so that the Oedipus complex soon assumes its classical form. The conflict takes on a more masculine and therefore more typical form in a son, whereas a daughter develops a specific linking for the father, with a correspondingly jealous attitude towards the mother. We could call this the Electra complex. As everyone knows, Electra took vengeance on her mother Clytemnestra for murdering her husband Agamemnon and thus robbing her – Electra – of her beloved father.

"Both these fantasy complexes become more pronounced with increasing maturity, and reach a new stage only in the postpubertal period, when the problem arises of detachment from the parents. This stage is characterized by the symbol we have already mentioned: the symbol of sacrifice. The more sexuality develops, the more it drives the individual away from his family and forces him to achieve independence."

The experience of separation from the parents of which Jung writes, is re-lived and resolved in every experience of separation from birth onwards. Therefore in the internal world, at every stage of development, psychological complexes manifest which have a corresponding image present in dreams and in creativity. These function as *daimones* i.e., significant nuclei, and function as a kind of guide for the individual. Regarding the roots of the uncontrolled and turbulent behavior of the adolescent, Fordham (1969) affirms that "these roots stem from the beginning of infancy, the period in which the mother, followed by the other members of the family constituted the whole of society for the child." (p. 120) In the first phases of maturity, the mother-child relationship is characterized by interdependence in which the baby looks for the function of nutrition and care from the mother. Today, the maternal function is increasingly being carried out also by the father, and when roles become less rigidly defined, the psychic functions from which the roles originate may grow confused. It is for this reason that it is during adolescence that parental figures have to be able to support the destructive dynamics that the adolescent puts into action in order to allow himself to separate from his parents. This symbolic "death" of his parents allows the youngster to grow through the means of the incest taboo, ending one situation and then being "reborn" into a new life. As I see it, a lack of this "passage" can lead to a fragility in the structure of the personality and can create serious pathology during development.

In Jungian thought, which is essentially operational and describes psychological functions and not psychic contents, the concept of personality and its creation is a dialectic process between oneself and the collective unconscious and between oneself and the collective consciousness. The family is the first and most important "social" place. This dialectic of the personality is set off by the necessity to differentiate oneself from the rest of reality and continually to define one's own identity, with regards to the unconscious psyche and the external world.

In adolescence, personal structures once again come into the spotlight, in relation to collective roles that now have to be made concrete. Omnipotent fantasies originate from the period of manic infantile defense, a period when heroes and heroines are formed, and are manifested in violent attacks against the parents and against society. Schizoid episodes, manifestations of depression, depersonalization and hysteria are also quite common at this age. The violence of these states is proverbial and when it starts to take hold, the young person needs a "holding" similar to that which the mother provided for her small child. A free and protected space, such as that which Dora Kalff has illustrated in sandplay therapy. This therapy has the capacity of containing aggression without its being auto-destructive: it allows the adolescent to experiment with his or her internal tensions, destructive and constructive, which can then be mediated and transformed.

Scars

Many experiences of this period hurt and leave scars that remain throughout adult life, interior lacerations that result from abruptly breaking away from previous situations. Separations – evolutionary processes of detachment from being a child and moving toward adulthood – often take the form of extreme heroes and heroines (heroes of war, violence, drugs, fast riding on motorbikes, alcohol abuse, anorexic/bulimic control over the body). On the one hand, these processes favor collective initiation rituals; on the other, they distance the individual from reflection and reintegration – with the result of separating parts of the Self. Extreme religious choices and ascetic practices express the motif of sacrifice very well. This is the first major conflict that one meets on the road to adulthood within our system of relationships that have something to do with the redemption of dependence. This psychic operation requires the sacrifice of the immediate pulsating response to open oneself up to the reflective and meditative activity between the internal and external world. This redemption brings with it the demolition of the figure of the parents, on which our own individual existence depends. Frequently, adolescents are not conscious of the human destiny which demands the painful abandonment of the parental figures to enter into the adult world. They continue perpetually to "save" these parental figures within the Self and thereby sacrifice their own independence. This sacrifice impedes development and leaves the individual feeling a failure with regards to the function of self-management.

At this point, the main problem that I find is that of helping the individual to stay faithful to his or her life-project of being able to cope with dark internal tensions. The failure to do so brings the risk that the individual may be overwhelmed by his own experiences and lose his identity, declining into himself. In this way, he resolves suffering by putting his own identity into a socially pre-defined scheme. The challenge of the young person is that of governing oneself, managing the relationship with oneself and with the external world, as a subject and as an object. Jung (1912) remarks: "The natural course of life demands that the young person should sacrifice his childhood and his childish dependence on the physical parents, lest he remain caught body and soul in the bonds of unconscious incest." (CW, paragraph 80, p. 356). Jung (1913) also considers the image of sacrifice to mean the renunciation of all infantile desires, which are more of an obstacle to the acquisition of the new in psychological adaptation than a fixation on the old or on past behavior.

At times, sacrifice expresses itself in primitive contents linked with the figure of the hero, i.e. images of death, courageous battles, abandonment and loss; such images appear in dreams, drawings and sandplay images and all throughout the imagination, and they constitute a source of conflict and disturbance. Such images can be active at an unconscious level, where images of death such as the killing of one's parents aim to make conscious and favor the elaboration of the end of infancy as a stage of life. This experience can cause suffering and desperation in the adolescent, and can effectively lead to the performance of acts of self-immolation, as in the omnipotence of anorexia, or in suicide. In these cases, the subject has not made conscious the dialectic symbolism of opposites, which instead permit evolution. The complementary theme, that of the sacrifice of others (in general the parents), brings with it mechanisms of projection of the individual's own regressions onto other people. These regressions (and the people onto whom they are projected, who are usually the individual's actual parents) cannot be overcome and are attacked, often very dramatically, by the individual himself. The incapacity to distinguish what their parents actually are from what they represent – the incapacity to distinguish what they can and cannot control regarding the management of themselves – highlights once more the incapacity to carry "the cross" of existence, which, on one hand is tension, and on the other, is the road to salvation and evolution, necessary for the growth of the young person.

The course of evolution, represented by the symbol of the cross, is well expressed in the figure of Christ who also carried the cross of existence from the moment of birth. He coherently followed his own personal path in life (many times), which meant leaving his parents and his birthplace, and overcame all challenges that could have made him regress to dependency of the dark and unconscious sides of himself. Supported by his faith in the Father and his trust in his own *daimon*, which here represents the support of our own intimate resources, like a guardian angel that holds us up, Christ remains coherent until sacrifice, which doesn't result from any failure of the Self, and instead takes place in the name of his love for others (which symbolically represents overcoming reference to one's own ego and the regressed incestuous desires represented by the religion of the Father).

In the parable of the prodigal son (Luke, 15,10), the father loves the youngest son, even though he is not trustworthy, and allows himself to be killed by him (Father, give me my part of inheritance). The Father, that is, Christ, loves the son up to the point that he accepts being unconsciously killed by him, many times. In this way, Christ was sacrificed because his behavior was foolish and his eldest son (in an imaginary follow-on from the parable) should have stopped the father, who was crazy for the love of his (weaker) youngest son. In the reconstruction of history, the Pharisees (older brothers) sent their father to the cross.

The Death and Re-Birth of Eros

At eighteen years of age, Eros, in his attempt to separate himself from his symbiotic relationship with his mother, had a psychotic breakdown: it was characterized by voices of conflicting spiritual entities (one good, the other evil) and by attempts to fulfill the gesture of sacrifice by throwing himself under a car, pushed by the negative voice in his head. His mother had been abandoned by her husband not long after Eros was born. The father was simultaneously expecting a child by another woman. Having being abandoned, the mother had dedicated herself to this god of passionate love who was Eros. (This is the patient's real name, and he has given me authorization to cite it in this work.) He was the only fruit of the relationship that had unexpectedly come to nothing. After the first appearance of his illness, Eros lived a frenzied existence, not accepting any proposed therapies and living in the maternal home without ever going out, because the external world was negative and persecutory.

I met Eros at the onset of his illness, when, having left the ward for intensive care, he was admitted to the psychiatric ward where I worked. He spoke very little, giggled and looked sideways; he seemed to be plagued with hallucinations but did not express them, because they were not experienced in an integrated way within his personality.

For this reason, he did not accept therapy and lived for approximately five years at home, inverting night and day and talking to himself, going out without being seen. Every now and again he came to meetings only with me and did not accept any other proposal which the psychiatric team suggested. He was admitted to the psychiatric ward another two times for the worsening of psychotic symptoms and with a diagnosis of paranoid schizophrenia. After about one year, I moved to another city and transferred to another hospital. I said goodbye to Eros with a sense of sadness because I realized how difficult it was for him to be treated by other colleagues. After a few years, he phoned me (also because his mother had encouraged him to do so) and came to my clinic, at first just for social meetings, and then he started a course of analysis. His analysis continued regularly for about three years and was carried out through the sandplay therapy. The unresolved problems of infancy in Eros manifested during the period of middle adolescence, a period when ideals, the need to belong to groups, and the struggle for autonomy are major issues. As we have seen, these are elements which are present along with others in the development of young people. For Eros, his lack of a father, his exclusive relationship with a mother who had been suddenly abandoned and who had to attempt to fulfill paternal as well as maternal functions, his instinctual drives and his mechanisms of primitive defense all converged and found expression in the fragility of the cohesion of the Self, and also in the strength of the Id as the boy was faced with the challenge of entering the social dimension on possibly autonomous terms. At the beginning of adolescence, Eros had started to study regularly and had then begun to work at the age of fifteen. In general, he had good relationships with his friends even without having had any significant emotional relationships. Towards sixteen years of age, he joined Japanese religious groups and, with his old friends, dreamed of a trip to Ireland, a land of myths and magic. Two years later, his friends decided to leave and they all met up in Belfast. They began working and found a house. He suggested that he join them and as the decision drew closer, his fears transformed into spiritual entities which oscillated between good and evil and which gradually expressed thoughts. These thoughts soon became voices, at first internal and then external. The voices talked to him and got louder and louder. The tension and the fear of breaking the ties to the mother, who would probably have felt abandoned yet again, promoted mechanisms of identity dispersion and fragmentation of the Self. Leaving for Ireland was like abandoning his mother, and in doing this Eros would have done exactly what his father had done. At the height of the tension, the voice ordered him categorically to throw himself beneath a speeding car because "we come from dust and to dust we will return."

When Eros came to my analytic studio for the first time, he was in a phase of imbalance. I now think his refusal to see anyone other than me had something to do with his having established a relationship with me which was based upon a silent understanding, ever since the first episode of his illness. Eros started by telling me about his dreams with images which were totally separate from each other. Religious symbols appeared, such as the cross, alongside a scene of dismemberment and violence. After about a year, while I myself was following the terminal phases of my father's illness, in the days in which he was dying and I was distraught, Eros went to the sandpit, looked at it and asks me something about the sand and the figurines.

During the first session with the sand, he says "I like making pyramids, I would like to make a sphinx" (he talks out loud as he works with the sand).

Figure I

This archaic symbol represents the beginning of the world according to oriental tradition. The pyramid built within a circle represents the possibility of a feeling that embraces the tomb of the father archetype. If the personal father is not present, an archetypal father can be constellated. Once we have resolved the pre-Oedipus problem, we can ask the maternal power (represented by the sphinx) to make up for the distance from the father. The square represents the father who tries to emerge from the "circle" of the maternal. The fear of losing oneself in the undifferentiated is presented here. In Tibetan mandalas, the square inside the circle represents all that comes before separation. The separation of the square from the circle (evident in the sandplay image) shows that we can conclude that there is a sense of Self and of other – a prerequisite for every possible evolution.

With a long release anti-psychotic drug, which he wants me personally to give him by means of a monthly injection, Eros accepts the therapy. The loss of my own father also opened me up to a new relationship with him that presented itself and evolved through my dreams during the course of the years. The capacity of being able to ally myself with the psychotic patient, sharing parts of my own life experiences, facilitated an empathetic channel that would otherwise not be utilized through verbal and cognitive content alone. In my experience, it is very frustrating and sterile to work in a cognitive-behavioral setting with schizophrenic patients where rules or treatments do not allow, through symbolic dimensions, access to a transitional area which is comprehensible to both patient and therapist.

In the second sandplay picture the car starts out from where we are. New energy has emerged from our relationship allowing him to move forward from out of the archaic image of before.

Figure 2

The car represents a major autonomy of Self that permits him to go forward in life. The car is no longer a source of death, as in the suicide of some years before, but an instrument of a new life.

The next session brings a dream:

> I was with a group of boys, we were going for a job and there were other people there. I had an interview with a large robust man. We had to produce objects within a set time, the more we produced, the more money we earned. We accepted, and then he arrived with an injection. He had to give us the injection, because otherwise we couldn't work.

The robust man represents a masculine power that can help the boys achieve autonomy – which is represented by the collective sense of production tied to the male world (which helps one achieve separation from the mother archetype). The job was possible, thanks to the injection. This modality of work goes back to *homo faber*, i.e. to the man who is bound to the profits of consumer production (which is an alienating modality of work but necessary in order to arrive at a higher level of existence). The dream is more personal than the sandplay image and also more direct and concrete, indicating that the work should go ahead thanks to the injection. Eros still needs to be recognized and supported, because by himself he is not able, he needs a strong man. He then does the third sandplay image, and while constructing it he says beneath his breath "the Chinese Wall." (Figure 3)

Then he talks about Roberto Benigni's film *La Vita è Bella*. The pyramid is transformed into an island in the shape of an arrow pointing towards a new direction with respect to the continent. We can also see the opposites – the whale and the dolphin – which respectively represent the mother and the autonomy of the child.

Figure 3

There is also a shark which could represent aggression towards the mother. When a dolphin appears in the sand for the first time in sessions with patients who are seriously disturbed, this is a positive prognostic indicator: the dolphin is the mammal that helps the man who is in difficulty (and in Russia it represents a good omen of new birth). The Chinese Wall represents the fact that new defenses between inside and outside are being built up (defenses that come from as far away as the Orient, and which are therefore archaic, but nonetheless sufficient to protect what lies within them).

In the fourth session of sandplay therapy, a new emotion appears and is shown by red rain and by the colors of the butterfly. (Figure 4)

Figure 4

The lion (he tells us) simultaneously represents the Self and aggression which now has been isolated (on an island), thus permitting other parts of the personality to remain together, thanks to the octopus. The last two images are images of movement where, from a central point, "arms" depart, which then circle and break, fragmenting and then reforming, imitating a process of reintegration of parts of the Self and of successive reintegrations. They are reminiscent of a swastika.

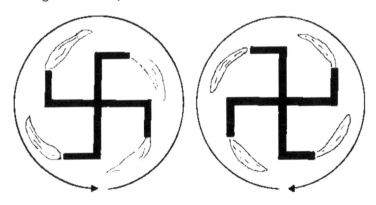

The swastika is a symbol which precedes the cross in the history of humanity, and it is often a type of garland that turns toward the wind.

The next image shows a winged horse.

Figure 5

Pegasus was born out of the death of the Gorgon, who was killed by Perseus, i.e. he was born from a negative situation (the mother is seen as negative). Then a god appears (Zeus), who expresses a new masculine energy which is positive and no longer tied to the negative mother. The Mexican (as Eros himself recounts) is present, and yet is not present. The Mexican is an aspect of the Id which is more personal than the previous images of the Self.

Passing on to the next sandplay image, the Chinese Wall appears, and finally the function of the warrior appears in Eros along with the masculine capacity to differentiate oneself from others, and to fight. The warrior hero takes on the responsibility of the risk of death, a risk that indicates the possibility of no longer being afraid of differentiating oneself from the unconscious. The fragility which is still present is expressed by the blue of the background on which the Chinese Wall is erected.

Figure 6

The scene is still unfinished. Eros from this point onwards accepts, being better structured, the assistance of the public psychiatric service within a project for rehabilitation and job placement. He agrees to the oral administration of atypical neuroleptics that improve ulterior negative symptoms, and he is likewise willing to see a psychiatrist who works with the community service. He goes out with his friends, sleeps regularly at night and starts to see his father, whom he has not seen for many years (thanks also to the support and mediation of a social worker). Every so often, he goes to work with him, plays football and joins in with day center activities. He also continues to see me, telling me about his dreams and unraveling images in the sand.

The last four sandplay sessions occurred approximately fourteen months after the first sessions, and are indications of how Eros would be during the phase of leaving the archetypal yoke of the undifferentiated, which had sacrificed him on the cross of death without any hope of escape.

In the next sandplay image, a current is contained in a triangular sea, where a dragon is present at the center.

Figure 7

Eros says that this is the Bermuda Triangle. The sea narrows, and around it are land and the continent: "Every time I come I never really know what to do. When I paint walls, the work is done and complete. Here with the sand, it's different. I now accept myself more as a person, I feel myself in movement,

I take life with a more philosophical approach. If something goes wrong for me, I think about it philosophically. I experience something different." The triangle, in this case, means a mysterious place where one may lose oneself in the psychotic experience. All the elements of the sea, voracious or mysterious, flow around the dragon. The appearance of the dragon in this ambivalent way, represents both the negative aspect and the transformative element: once one has faced it, one is able to overcome the negative energies. In Eros, these images probably reactivate positive and heroic parts of himself which were previously hidden and suppressed. An Id that is more conscious than its obscure sides – the hole of the Bermuda Triangle of his unconscious – can now permit him to face the climb back up towards a more integrated existence.

In the following sandplay image, energy circulates and moves toward a goal, which is a mountain with trees, to which cars are directed.

Figure 8

In the next sandplay image, Eros tells us that this is a house. This is where the first human figures appear (even though infantile) and this expresses personality – with its own spaces, even if they are tight and maze-like.

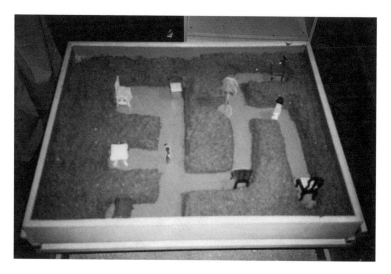

Figure 9

And lastly: the image of a football match. This is when Eros announces to me that he has found a job, and also when he communicates to me (not verbally) that an impersonal arche-typal principle has made itself human.

The purpose of the game is to allow conflict to express itself socially within the rules and limits of a possible new existence. Once sacrifice has been made, it enters into social life and becomes a part of it. Having shared a clinic with my father, who was a homeopathic doctor, I too had had to endure a period of separation and social redefinition when he died.

Figure 10

During his course of sandplay therapy, Eros created primordial shapes such as the circle and the square, which then entered into movement. These then transformed into the swastika with four arms which broke up in successive images. Some moths later, he reconstructed it, and it appears in the image of the mountain which represents verticality and the possible "climb back up."

In the final image of the football game, the conflicts within him could coexist without destroying each other. This was shown as the two opposing teams of the football match, which were in opposition for the purpose of the game. During the process of his use of images, Eros thus made use of the principle symbols that come to us from tradition, of the signs that have been left to us by the development of humanity itself. The swastika is the primordial symbol which precedes the cross, and it has the same meaning in the history of humanity. It is the third of four fundamental symbols, including the circle and the square. The cross appears in Eros' sandplay images in the form of the swastika and also in some of his dreams where a number of crosses are placed in such a way as to form a circle. The cross in fact obeys a well defined relationship with the other symbols: the intersection of the two lines meets at the center, which opens outwards, making a circle which then divides into four parts. The square and the triangle can also be formed from the cross by connecting the four lines that form it. Like the square, the cross represents the earth and is charged with subtle, intermediate and dynamic characteristics. The symbolism of the square is linked to that of the cross, insofar as the design of the cross plays with the relationship of the internal parts of the square (which are also similar to those of the cross). The cross takes on the meanings of spatial orientation, of animals and also of storms, and it stands in relation to the transcendental. It combines within itself the functions of synthesis and measurement, and joins the earth to the sky, commingling space and time. It is the symbol of mediation and of communication, it is diffusion and emanation, but also collection and recapitulation.

Eros threw himself to the ground in his sacrifice of himself; he internally fulfilled a new symbolic sacrifice with his non-verbal analytic work in the sand. Seven years after his breakdown, he was able to reintegrate those parts of himself which had been shattered and fragmented. This allowed him to take up a life of adaptation and relationships. For a psychotic subject, the opportunity to access a channel of non-verbal communication where cognitive distortions and emotional conflicts can be expressed symbolically, as in sandplay therapy, is a road to the integration of parts which would otherwise be difficult to reach in the course of psychotherapy.

References

Fordham, M. (1969) *Children as Individuals*, London: Hodder and Stoughton.

Jung, C. G. (1912) CW, Vol. 5, VIII, "The Sacrifice." Princeton: Princeton University Press.

Jung, C. G. (1913) CW, Vol. 4 II, "The Theory of Psychoanalysis." Princeton: Princeton University Press.

Jung, C. G. (1930) CW, Vol 8, VI, "The Stages of Life." Princeton: Princeton University Press.

Images of Time: New Departures at a Public Drug Addiction Clinic

Marcella Merlino

> *Quid est ergo tempus? Si nemo ex me quaerat scio;*
> *si quaerenti explicare uelim, nescio.*
>
> What, then, is time? If no one asks me, I know
> what it is. If I wish to explain it to him who asks
> me, I do not know.
>
> Saint Augustine
Confessions, XI, 14

"My head's hung up on time."

André seemed curious as well as amused when I suggested that he try this new method. But in our following meetings he left aside the idea of working with sand, and for several days never returned to the subject. Then, however, he stopped me in the hallway, to ask: "So, how about it? When are we going to work with sand? You've made me curious." It was only outside the setting that he managed to express some measure of interest, and once inside the "sand room" he revealed his great embarrassment. He giggled and attempted to avoid the situation, but on being reminded that he had to choose a single sandbox, and that he had to do what he wanted to do within the space of forty-five minutes, he also grumbled "that's what's so unfair." Then he chose to work in the box where the sand was dry, and remarked: "Everything here is calm and bright, so I like it more. The wet sand there in the other box is dark and messy, much too messy." And once having finished his work, he looked for excuses to remain in the room, to the point of my finally having to ask him explicitly to leave, while assuring him again and again of the date and time for his next appointment. But he stayed in the building – which is something, moreover, he would often do – wandering around the halls and talking with the doctors on duty about his new experience, up until closing time.

At the next appointment he spoke more boldly: "It's just not fair," he began, "and first of all for the time limit. I come in here and want to do my work and then you say that after an hour I have to leave...."

Me: "But that's no different from the meetings when you come to have a talk with me ..."

André: "In fact, I don't even like it then!"

Me: "But on the other hand, it's a way of being fair to everybody, to you and to everybody else. Everybody has their own hour. And you can all be sure that during that hour you won't be disturbed."

André, nodding: "That's true too." But then, after a pause, he continued, "But it's still not right. It just shouldn't be that way. I go ahead and make an image, and then you destroy it..."

Me: "That's true, but I also take photos of what you've done."

Andrea: "A photo's not the same. And what if I don't get done? You set a time, and when it's up I have to go, even if I haven't finished."

Me: "You can pick it up again at the next session."

André: "But how can I pick it up again, if I can't return to the same sandobx I was working on before?"

Me: "You can't go back to the same construction, but you can pick up the same story, the same theme. The next time you come here, you can always go back to the same idea as the time before."

André: "That's not the same."

Me: "Try to think of a comic strip. Every panel is a separate drawing. But the story consists of all the panels taken together. What we do here is a bit like that. Every image is a piece of a story that's concerned with you, and you're the story teller. And the story takes on meaning when everything's taken together. At the end, if you like, you'll be able to put together all the various panels by way of my photos of the things you've done in the sand, comparing them, and reading them perhaps as a sequence, the one following the other."

The idea of the "comic strip" seemed to convince him. "Okay," he said, "let's give it another try." Rising to his feet, he asked, "Aren't you coming with me?" He took off his jacket and turned toward the sandboxes, which were both right there, ready and waiting.

While looking at the boxes and trying to decide which of the two he would use, André remarked to himself: "Let's do something simple. Something really simple. A story that's clear and simple." A short while later, he picked up a jeep and used it to replace a smaller car which he'd placed on a tortuous path that he'd shaped with his hands in the wet sand. As he worked he kept on making comments, always speaking out loud while talking with himself; he also kept an eye on the shelves, where a variety of objects were clearly in view. "If I wait, I'll find the right thing. But my head's hung up on time."

André, at thirty-six years old, had been coming to our clinic since 1982. He had been on various methadone programs, which administer progressively smaller doses of the drug, and he had often flanked such treatments with individual and family meetings with psychologists. He had often interrupted his programs, just as he had often changed psychologist. In the course of the last three years, his abuse of drugs and alcohol had considerably diminished, step by step with his greater progress in the various work and study projects he had managed to undertake, and little by little to conclude, with considerable effort and commitment.

So, when I suggested that André work with sand, that wasn't his first experience with psychological therapy. Yet there were certain doubts and fears of which now he seemed to grow aware for the very first time. It was the very first time he realized that psychotherapeutic work obeys a rhythm all its own, and that such an experience has a time dimension. Each session is of limited, finite duration, just like the size of the sandbox, which has physical measurements in which one has to remain. And by way of the perception that photographs could allow him to "fix" a memory of the psychotherapeutic process, André became somehow able to contain the anxieties connected with moments in time that seemed, within his fantasies, to vanish into the void. ('When the session is over,' he had seemed to ask, 'what will happen to the parts of myself which I have thrown out into it? Will they be destroyed?') André, indeed, seemed little by little to establish a fertile contact with his resistance to the realization that a process of evolution has a discontinuous dimension in time, or a pulse-like beat of sessions and suspensions. He began to see that the time that passed during moments of suspension didn't have to undo the efforts and progress already made, just as the time spent in sessions could never exhaust the efforts and progress that possibly might be made. Quite to the contrary, he had to see that the final result lay in the interplay of these two moments, or in all of their various occurrences finally taken together.

Clearly enough, this reflection was only beginning: André still experienced the passage of time as a kind of threat: "My head's hung up on time." But the notion that haste can be deleterious seemed slowly to make its advance "If I wait, I'll find the right thing."

"You can't tell an addict to wait."

It seems to me that the Self began to discover these new resources as a result of the stimulus of working with sand. And the stimulation of such results is one of the most frequent and interesting capabilities that sandplay therapy seems to display when employed with patients addicted to drugs.

It was in 1995 that Rome's Public Clinic for the Treatment of Drug Addiction, where I am currently employed, first set up a room for Sandplay therapy, and this initiative (which in Italy was entirely unprecedented) derived from the desire to offer an alternative to exclusively verbal therapy to a category of patients who are notoriously recalcitrant to psychotherapy. Finally, however, I believe that its introduction into a public clinic for the treatment of drug addiction was a step that led me to a deeper understanding of one of the most particular features of the pathology of drug addiction: I came to a greater understanding of the extent to which the addict's relationship with time plays a fundamental role in his or her history of drug abuse, and this allowed me to set up a clinical approach that's capable of intervening with a certain efficacy.

The therapeutic setting is known in fact to be quite difficult with such patients. Their tendency to interrupt therapy doesn't allow the continuity which the therapeutic setting requires, and their urgent demand to have everything without delay hampers the construction of a therapeutic alliance, just as it can even disrupt the delivery of pure and simple social and medical assistance.

Working with patients who're addicted to drugs means that one has to be willing to confront their sense of time, and the rhythms they in fact impose. One has to know that the therapeutic relationship will suffer interruptions and resumptions; as well one has to be ready to deal with the emotions and the sense of urgency that the drug-addicted patient not only expresses on his own, but also unleashes in the minds and feelings of those whose task is to offer him assistance. One has to come to terms, in short, with all of the addict's "altered rhythms."

The dimension of time has for many years been a central theme of my professional practice with drug-addicted patients. It was also the subject, in 1991, of a special research project[1] that analyzed the statements and case histories of younger heroin addicts in the care of our Public Clinic; the goal of the study was to reach a better understanding of "the symbolic scenarios in which drug addiction situates itself and, in its own particular way, constructs." (Merlino and Padiglione 1995: 109) And one of the very first things to be clearly seen was the centrality and singularity of the experience of the dimension of time in the lives of young drug addicts (see also Charles-Nicolas 1981), even if this condition doesn't meet necessarily with awareness or expression on the part of the various social forces that are also called into play.

The experience of time is clearly one of the central issues in all pathologies. One must only, for example, remember how patients feel themselves to be "trapped," or "blocked," and incapable of moving forward. But drug addiction has a special feature all its own: the addict moves constantly back and forth between the heroin "rush" and the re-emergence of craving, and thus lives out a dramatic accentuation of the experience of the passing of time. Addicts are also prone to a decidedly manipulatory or instrumental use of their pathology. The addict sets off any number of levels of cultural and relational conflict with respect to notions of time and the ways in which we use and respect it. For example, the addict demands that his methadone be supplied immediately, just as he'll demand the instantaneous delivery of a certificate he needs to possess. In both situations, the addict is "deploying" the same mode of behavior – the same sense of "haste" – that guides his search for heroin throughout the city streets. The addict knows that such behavior delivers responses that sweep away all requests for patience; and he also knows, more than anything else, that it confirms his classification as an addict, and thus as a person whose sense of urgency is always justified: "You can't tell an addict to wait."[2]

Background studies reveal that heroin addiction is generally the culmination of a whole series of risky games that generally begin with adolescence (see De Leo 1982). And it's a question of games in which the dimension of time, combined with transgression and risk, is a fundamental element. Everything is staked on a single instant: in the young man's imagination, everything is concentrated into a single moment. The prize if the game is won – in this adolescent system of belief – is the acquisition of character (see Goffmann 1972).

Night-time joyrides after leaving the discotheque, speeding in the wrong direction through one-way streets, ignoring the red of traffic lights. Quickly scrawling one's name or monogram on the side of a train or a wall. Hurling stones from an overpass at cars speeding unawares along the highway below. These are dares that some young men all too frequently accept without hesitation. Even if very different in terms of style and the kinds of danger with which they play, all of these games are characterized by a crucial factor of time.

The Moment of Truth vs. Flat Routine

The core of these games is always the attempt to "personalize" one's time, and thus to escape the monotony of a daily life which is felt to be alien, impoverished and humiliating. Adult time, as seen by such young men, is flat "routine," and their goal is to supplant it with a time of their own, attempting "to capture the moment" and to make it a "moment of truth," charged with high emotion. But if the game with drugs makes itself a consistent part of the young man's life, the "moment of truth" then gradually transforms into another desperate, degrading routine. And even if the addict denies this fact with all his strength, even if for years he persists in insisting on his freedom from any sort of dependence, while at the very same time on a constant search for still other "moments of truth" (a marriage, a child, some challenging line of work) through which to exit from drugs and their routine, this is the point at which he generally makes his first attempt to seek out help.

My own experience also shows me that the addict continues to view himself in terms of this opposition even inside the therapeutic relationship. The addict continues to oscillate between the hope for a "moment of truth," and a collapse into "flat routine." Interruptions, urgencies and cyclic repetitions, impelling requests and episodes of sudden flight, no less than the alternate devaluation and idealization of the relationship all belong to a series of defenses that derive from the way the patient relates to the experience of time.

The difficulties faced by therapists and social workers who operate in such contexts are more than clear: the requests they're attempting to satisfy are always impelling, but always at the very same time on the verge of being withdrawn.

But I discovered sandplay therapy to constitute an alternative. Colorful, absolutely unexpected, practical, visual, photographable, and not necessarily verbal, it offered many addicted patients a special sensation. It was able, even in very brief periods, and even at times in a single session, to give them the feeling of having come into contact with something they had never known before, and with something truly important (see also Ammann 1991). And when working with patients who offer no assurance that they'll return for their next appointment, it's essential to be able to make some sort of progress in the brevity of the here and now.

"My hands knew I had only just begun"

So, questions and reflections which have never before been dealt with begin to surface. And the patient little by little perceives that meaningful traces of his day-to-day life and interior experience find formulation in the images which he leaves behind in the sand. This, in fact, is the way in which it seems to me that addicts who work with sandplay therapy manage to make first contact with their relationship to the experience of time, which ranks as one of the crucial features – crucial though far from all-embracing – of their many-sided pathology.

The work that's done through sandplay therapy can of course be read in many different ways, and at many different levels, all of which have to be held in mind if the work is fully to be understood. But for the patients I myself have followed, and continue to follow, with the help of the sand and the sandbox and the way their hands delve into them, I'd say that they often give the impression of having made first contact with a whole new dimension of time. They begin to relate to a dimension of time that belongs to the hands that compose their scenes, and which in doing so become vehicles of emotions, desires, and memories. As one session follows the other, the patients learn to listen to their hands, nearly as though understandng that their hands possess a knowledge from which they have something to learn. They learn to accept a relationship to time which differs entirely from the one that brought them to me, and which frequently still conditions their lives once they have left my room. They discover a dimension of time that accepts no orders and obey no commands, and where every attempt to speed things up is experienced as constrictive and out of place. "You have to have time to be able to construct something. Trying to do things fast makes me make mistakes." "I thought I had finished, but my hands knew I had only just begun." "Something's missing; I can't quite say what; I have to look for it…. There, that's the way it's supposed to be. And now, yes, now I've finished." This is "the patient's time," and the therapist has no control of it. It's not the therapist who makes the suggestion that the moment has come for the patient to rise from his chair and to plunge his hands into the sandbox; or to stroke the sand with his fingertips; or to walk over to the shelves and take a careful look at them, running his eyes across them until finding the "right" object; or to stop because he "feels" that his work with the sand has reached some kind of conclusion. It's the patient's hands themselves that lead back to a past that suddenly, as though by magic, returns to the surface, with spontaneous and pleasurable communications. The scenes the patients construct are charged with experiences connected to memory, which is all the more surprising since memories only rarely appear in their narratives about themselves, so much so as to make one fear that all important memories may have gone entirely lost.

The Recovery of Memory: "… my grandfather was a fisherman …"

Giuseppe constructs a rural landscape, and, on the right, digs down in the sand to the point of revealing the blue on the bottom of the sandbox, thus forming a lake. At its edge he places a fisherman with a fishing rod that he himself had constructed with a stick of wood and a piece of string. He comments: "I love to go fishing. Especially at night, in the sea, when everything's so quiet. My grandfather taught me how to fish. He was a fisherman. As well as a hunter. But, for me, I don't like to hunt. Killing animals is ugly. With fish things seem more even. My father, on the other hand, doesn't have the patience for fishing. He likes to hunt."

On another occasion, he represents a town on a special feast day, with a couple of newlyweds just coming out of the church, to the music of an organ grinder. He then remembers a trip he made to Holland, where he saw an organ grinder with a pet monkey that collected money from passers-by. There's also a town band in the scene he constructs, as in every self-respecting small-town festival. He tells me about his father and the town in which he lives and the music school he'd have liked to attend, in a free, spontaneous flow of associations.

Giuseppe next returned to the sandbox on the day after his birthday, which once again, for the first time in years, he'd celebrated with his father, whose birthday was the same as his own. He built what he called an "Astrological Temple," with rays of sunshine peeping through slits between great blocks of stone. There were numerous archeological sites everywhere around it, with workmen digging and finds that once discovered were carefully stored and preserved. While looking for objects that struck his fancy, and developing the notion of a "civilization more ancient than Rome, but so advanced as to know how to measure time and predict the eclipses of the sun and moon, which is why they built their Temple to the Sun," he told me about the gifts he'd received and given, and also about the coincidence that he and his father were both born on March 19, which is father's day. At the end of the session, looking with satisfaction at what he had done, he commented: "We're only at the very beginning. There's still so much work to do, hunting down the finds that have to be brought to light."

In combination with the classical archaeological metaphor of the therapeutic process, so clearly evident in the scene with the Temple, Giuseppe's reflections on his birthday, on his father's birthday, and on father's day celebrations suggest the thought that the passage of time and the way it's called into view by the celebration of two birthdays that span two generations seems to unfold into a great pageant where a single scene holds a mysterious, grandiose past, an active present, and a future that remains to be discovered.

We know that the recovery of a personal identity which is based on the memory of one's own origins is normally promoted by sandplay therapy, and we see that this is also true for patients who're addicted to drugs. Sandplay therapy permits the therapist to offer the patient a visualization of his or her private world of symbolic images, and the stable, concrete form of these visualizations encourages the emergence of memory, and the ability to hold it in mind. And memory is of crucial importance for patients whose perceptions of everything are marked by urgency, distance and indifference.

Thanks to the memories evoked by the sandbox, and to the emotions that little by little emerge from them, the drug-addicted patient begins to construct a narrative that tells his story, and which otherwise remains unthinkable. The addict overcomes the interruptions which are typical of all his attempts at therapy, but owing not so much to any development that keeps him from skipping sessions, than to the fact that the scarlet thread of his story can at any moment be rediscovered. His reflections are no longer centered entirely on the abuse of heroin or giving it up, on methadone or the pains of withdrawal. There's finally an end to the constant repetition of things connected with current trials and circumstances, and so often declared and repeated as no longer to hold any meaning, no less for the person who's listening than for the person who's doing the talking. The patient abandons the mask that makes him no more than "a drug addict" whose behavior is always predictable and always stereotyped. He abandons that act of self-definition which constitutes the refuge for any number of young men who are afraid to face up to the world. Instead he enters the dimension of his own personal history, the history that makes him different from anyone and everyone else, and which, even by snatches of variable length, can always be more deeply explored.[3]

Both therapist and patient are enabled to feel that they've made the acquaintance of "slices of life" that, no matter how brief or fragmentary, can grow into a full-fledged narrative.

After the sandbox session in which he built his Temple, Giuseppe returned for a few more sessions, and then broke them off. He returned about a month later, and we worked for a while together, until he broke things off again. Later, however, he came back and remarked to me, "When I don't come, it's not that I want to call our meetings off. It's just that at times I feel the need to take a break, a need for a pause; but inside me

I know that it's only a question of time before I come back here again." That day, in the sand, he represented a prehistoric landscape, with a large central lake surrounded by vegetation, and also with dinosaurs and a prehistoric man, still with the features of an ape, who strode entirely naked towards his cave, and with the carcass of a hunted animal slung across his shoulder. "Now, this time, we're at twenty thousand years ago. We're in a past that's much more ancient that the time when I built the Temple in the sandbox," he remarked.

So, the process of "excavation," or "regression" had continued, in spite of Giuseppe's periodic habit of not showing up for our sessions.

The Recovery of Memory: "If my father had known ..."

Giuliano is forty years old and has four children, aged from four to eleven. He has been a drug addict for about twenty years. He has spent more time locked up than free, and last came out of jail a month ago, thanks to a law that offers addicts a program of rehabilitation instead of a prison term. In Giuliano's case, at his own request, the program provides for three weekly therapy sessions at a Community Treatment Center, with only sporadic control meetings at the Public Drug Addiction Clinic, in addition to being required to have regular urine examinations, to verify the absence of the use of psychoactive substances. But at his very first session at the Clinic, he was thoroughly seduced by the various materials he found on view. He was fascinated and asked for information, avidly observing the objects arranged on the shelves, and touching the sand in the sandboxes. Then, suddenly, he plunged his hands into the sand and divided it up into two parts, separated by a long split that revealed the blue bottom of the sandbox. He several times repeated, "I don't know why, but I want to divide the sand in two." He then remarked that he felt himself to be split into two different parts: the Giuliano who had been an addict for over twenty years and who now was living through a pause in his addiction, but who in fact didn't know what to do; the other part was the husband and father who had always shirked responsibility. He told me about his four children, "born by accident," and insisted he was tired of such a repetitious life, of always finding himself in jail, and of years that passed while never causing anything to change. He asked me then if he could come again to see me in the course of the following week, instead of after a month.

Figure 1

At the next session, he drew a profile of a face in the box with wet sand, a face with a cigarette in its mouth. He then explained that his father had always drawn that face on the steamed-up windows of the family kitchen when he and his brothers and sisters had been children. His father had been very authoritarian, and had beat them, but they respected him, and if he hadn't so dramatically died perhaps none of the three of them would ever have become a drug addict. "Or maybe so, you can never tell." The following week, Giuliano drew an image of a farm house in the sand, traced out with a stream of water on the sand in the dry sandbox (Figure 1, previous page), and this again took him back to his childhood: to the times in the summer when they had all returned to the south, to the village where Giuliano was born, and which the whole family had left behind. "That's where the best of my memories are all concentrated, when we'd roam the orchards, stealing figs. Nothing like this shitty life in Rome. If my father had known that he was coming here to die, hit by a car at a traffic light, he'd never have moved."

But Giuliano didn't show up for his next appointment, nor for the one that followed it. When he did come back, who knows, it may perhaps have been in compliance with an order from some court, which more or less forced him to do so. But he talked about the emptiness he felt inside himself, and how he tried to deal with it.

"The way you make use of your time is important. You get up in the morning, and don't know what to do, you don't know where to go. You just feel empty, and that's it. You don't know how to get organized. So, a fix first thing in morning, at eight o'clock, can look like a good idea, since then you'll be okay till noon: you just won't feel the emptiness, and you don't have to get organized. So that's why I always try to keep busy; I only do housework, but still it's a help. If I didn't have anything to do, it would all be over. But I'm going to have to find a job, something that gets me out of the house; I can't get by with only being able to stay off heroin by staying locked up in the house, or when I'm in jail. I have to learn to stay away from it out in the streets as well, to be able to walk away from it and go about my business."

He didn't work with the sand, or even look at the sandboxes or the shelves. But at the end of the session he remarked in a lowered voice, "I've been thinking about the sand these last few days. It's as though it took me back to things from before, a long way back. I don't know if times like that will ever be able to return. The time before I was twenty, when there were still no drugs. It made me a little sad to return to such clean memories, but perhaps they can give me a clearer look at what happened."

Memory, in Giuliano's case, was charged with regret for everything he'd lost, and which could never return. The pain aroused by his sense of impotence had been so strong as to lead him to abandon, at least momentarily, a road he had first begun to tread with great enthusiasm.

"My life is like a book of which I've always read only the first chapter."

I'd like to close these reflections with a few remarks on two sandbox constructions. In both of them, though in highly different ways, it seems to me that the experience of time has been given visibility.

The first is a representation of Castel Gandolfo (the small town outside of Rome, famous as the pope's summer residence) and has a round, central lake; the old part of the town is along its left edge, and the modern part – represented by a large hotel, and by a group of workers busy in the street – is on the lower right. At the top, in the middle, Antonio has set up rail-way tracks, rested on the sand and with neither beginning nor end. They do, however, carry a locomotive. Antonio remarked, "That's the station." He set up various people around the place, people walking back and forth, and one couldn't say where they might be going or perhaps have come from. "These people are tired; they're tourists," he explained, referring to a couple of puppets who had the air of being overheated. The figure with which he concluded his scene was a little man seated on a bench.

Antonio remarked, "My life is like a book of which I've always read only the first chapter." He was recounting his fights with Rita, and the way they made up as though nothing had happened, without emotion, without explanations, in a constant repetition of things he had already seen, and which I had already listened to.

His scene seems to me to render this sense of exhaustion, this movement that amounts to a kind of immobility, with startling vividness. Antonio's sandbox image allows him to talk about himself, and to offer a description of a way of life in which time appears to have stopped, as though blocked by events which can only repeat themselves. But while seeing this dimension of time appear beneath his eyes, he could little by little make contact with it, and thus was able to reach the point of discussing a number of experiences he'd never talked about before, and thus of abandoning, for the first time, the arid victimism through which he viewed himself.

The scene in Luciano's sandbox is very different, but no less conflictual. He has set up pairs of objects, one in front of the other, that represent oppositions: a vase of flowers and a shark; a sheep and a lion. At a certain point he was attracted by the figure of a werewolf (Figure 2) with a wide-open mouth that shows sharp teeth. The figure's hands are clawed and hairy, and he's using them to rip off his clothes – the clothes of an office worker, in suit and tie – thus revealing the bestial body that suddenly has burst into shape inside them. Luciano placed it in the sandbox, and turned it in my direction, as if it were a puppet that was standing on a stage and directing comments to an audience. But I had the impression of not being able to tell if the person talking were the puppet, or the puppeteer who remains in the wings. Luciano, in any case, looked me straight in the face and passionately defended the werewolf: "There are two totally different people inside the werewolf: the man and the wolf. And everybody is against him, he's seen as evil, as a creature who rips out people's throats. But I myself feel sorry for him. It's not his fault. If he's a wolf, he has to follow his instincts. Wolves kill rabbits and not human beings, and once they learn to recognize humans for what they are, they don't go anywhere near them. So if this is a man who turns into a wolf and therefore acts like one, killing rabbits and sheep, what's he doing that's so terribly wrong?"

Figure 2

Later, as he placed the symbols of the sun and the moon directly in front of each other, he remarked: "Only the sun and the moon owe no explanations to anybody. The one rises when the other sets…. There's nothing certain in the world we live in, except for the sun and the moon, and for time that passes, with nothing that's able to stop it…."

The cyclical nature of drug addiction is here summed up in a single image. The werewolf here is a symbol of the way in which the addict's periods of normalcy are suddenly and repeatedly devastated by the uncontainable explosion of a terrifying, bestial force; it's in the very same way that the addict passes from periods of holding drugs in check to others in which he loses all control.

Quite the opposite, the images of the sun and the moon refer, in Luciano's fantasy, to cyclic phenomena that lie beyond all judgment: they belong to an untouchable and immutable reality that offers reassurance and security, never in any danger of encountering obstacles along their road, and always as unreachable as dreams.

Antonio's story, like Luciano's, and those of many others as well, is a fabric of interruptions and of urgent, impelling needs: the sandbox, however, allowed them both to move forward along a path, and to start to face up to their disturbed experience of time.

Conclusions

Our Drug Addiction Clinic is a public service where clients come and go, and where their stories are "thrown on the table" without the attentions and finishings that characterize other settings, and especially the setting of private therapy; these stories, indeed, are most often heard – in situations where roles and spaces are highly confused – by a great variety of necessarily distracted ears, and often by persons who are overwhelmed by a crushing sense of impotence. Sandplay therapy, in such debilitating circumstances, seems to me to be able to represent an oasis: that new space which presents itself as both "free and protected" (Kalff 1980). It offers the experience of an intervisual and intersubjective context that's able to improve communication between therapist and addict. The addict is a patient with a grave, full-blown pathology that needs an adequate language through which to discover stimuli for processes of elaboration. And these are the terms on which the novel rhythms and motivations that come to the fore in the experience of playing with sand can turn into resources that the addict is somehow able to rediscover and put to use in the task of facing up to life.

Sandplay therapy, in my own experience, holds out the possibility of culling "slices" or "fragments" of life from the voices and hands of the patients who set to work in my room; and no matter how small these fragments at times may be, it offers the opportunity to reflect on them; and these reflections may perhaps be able in the future to open up new roads.

There can be no doubt that addicts are patients who present all sorts of obstacles – instability, impulsiveness, a notorious resistance to psychotherapeutic work, and a range of "altered" rhythms – which are hard to confront and overcome. It's also clear that such obstacles are justification for searching out routes which constitute alternatives to psychotherapy. But even if sandplay therapy doesn't do away with the difficulties that the heroin addict encounters in learning to give up drugs, and even if sandplay therapy, like every other therapy, is something from which patients can decide to flee, it seems to me nonetheless that those who come into contact with it enjoy the possibility of allowing themselves, by way of the images constructed during their sessions, to accept the kind of time dimension that offers a chance for a dialog with oneself.

Notes

[1] This research project was undertaken in collaboration with Vincenzo Padiglione, who holds the chair of Cultural Anthropology at the Psychology Department of Rome's La Sapienza University. See M. Merlino and V. Padiglione, 1995: 109-124.

[2] This phrase is often heard, and is even repeated by the patients themselves when they're forced to wait for anything, no matter if standing in line to receive their daily dose of methadone, or if waiting for their turn to enter the office of a social worker. It may even be used in the attempt to speed delivery of the session of psychotherapy that the patient himself requested only the day before. Patients in the care of drug addiction clinics quite normally couch requests for medical, psychological or social consultation in a tone of absolute urgency: it constitutes their standard mode of interpersonal relationship.

[3] James Hillman (1996) is no less dense than light in his reflections on the antidotes to be brought into play to liberate oneself from the syndrome of the victim, or on the notions of calling and individual destiny as the crucial themes of effective psychotherapy.

References

Ammann, R. (1991), *Healing and Transformation in Sandplay. Creative Processes Become Visible.* Chicago: Open Court.

Charles-Nicolas, A. J. (1981), "Il tossicomane e il tempo," *Documenti Cisf* 24, pp. 18-25.

De Leo, G. (1982), "Come la tossicodipendenza diventa devianza." In Gius, E. (ed), *La questione droga.* Milano: Giuffrè.

Goffmann, E. (1972), "Where the Action is?" in *Interaction Ritual.* London: Allen and Unwin.

Kalff, D. (1980), *Sandplay.* Boston: Sigo Press.

Merlino, M. and Padiglione, V. (1995), "Ritmi Alterati. La tossicodipendenza come disturbo della temporalizzazione" in *Psicologia Clinica* n. 2, Maggio-Agosto, pp. 109-124.

Sandplay and the Analytical Partnership

Franco Castellana

It is widely held concerning sandplay therapy that the support and encouragement of the patient's activities of representation in a free but protected space is in and of itself therapeutic. Such points of view primarily direct attention to the work the patient performs in the sandbox, and to how the sandbox presents itself as a powerful activator of the psyche's capacity to elaborate symbols, and thus of its powers of self-healing.

I myself am allied with those who maintain that sandplay can in no way be extrapolated from the context of the analytical process in which it takes place, and this is all the more evident with borderline cases and when dealing with elements of psychosis. For some years now my research has ever more centered on examining patients' sandbox "creations" for the emergence and concretization of a complex but efficacious intersection and integration of word and image, such as finally to be able to effect a transformation of the patient's psychic reality.

I stand at a certain remove from the various theories on the use of sandplay which stress the undoubtedly healing aspects of the emergence of images, since my experience in this regard has clearly been more problematic. In the course of my work I have unavoidably had to learn never to underestimate the particular intensity with which the patient's affects *precipitate* within the sandbox and then *drop their weight* on the partners in the analytical process. It is clear to me that the patient's "creations" in the sandbox are marked by a particularly powerful affective charge that intensely mobilizes and constellates *the analyst as much as the patient*. I insist on the fundamental premise that the sandbox mobilizes the patient's transference and the analyst's countertransference with equal intensity.

My thesis, from the point of view of the analytical partnership, is that the emergence of images in a field that encourages their representation does not necessarily, *per se*, bring about healing. The sandbox is able to mobilize charges of emotion which are often of great intensity, and this alone should make us see it as not only as a possible vehicle for the integration of highly significant psychic elements (especially with respect to dynamics of transference and countertransference, which then must be properly dealt with in the analytical setting), but also as the origin of a possible impasse, when it activates the analyst's Shadow.

My work with sandplay therapy has revealed it to be a source of particularly meaningful moments of transformation, and of equally radical difficulties in cases in which the sandbox images (and the patient's behavior with respect to them) constellate the analyst's unconscious, and especially so when the patient communicates an aggressiveness of which the destructive valences are particularly intense. In the latter case, the analyst who has chosen to use the sandbox in the analytical setting, and whose personal predispositions lead him to experience the sandbox as a physical extension of his own body, may find himself inclined to defend himself from the patient's destructive drives. This leads in turn to a possible reduction of the analyst's sensibility and perceptual faculties, and at times to true and proper blindness to precisely the *most powerful* elements which the patient brings up. The resultant impasse in the analytical relationship may even at times lead patients to interrupt analysis, owing to the feeling of finding it impossible to find a place for their destructive drives, either within or outside of themselves.

Jung's "Answer to Job"[1] has been of particular aid in shaping my reflections on this subject. As in all of his work, he doesn't pursue his theme in a linear way: as his principal argument develops, he progressively flanks it with others. And while we seem to see some of his thoughts as the immediate and logical outgrowth of those that come before them, others inexplicably bloom and wither in the space of just a few lines. So, it's far from surprising, here again, in the midst of a dense and fascinating discourse, to see Jung at times deliver himself of what today we at best might call "strong statements."

Jung, as I see it, addresses the heart of the matter when he makes the assertion, "His encounter with His creature changes the creator."[2]. The meaning and *raison d'etre* of such a statement lie in all the various vicissitudes of this story of God, His Shadow, and His "creature" Job. But the story's implications and the issues it raises are easily found to extend beyond the frame of reference in which we originally find them.

At the metapsychological level, the story's most immediate implications might reside in the fact that it's only by way of a confrontation with Job, who is both the Ego and Ego-consciousness, that an archetype (which could even, as I see it, be the archetype of the Self) proves capable of growing "conscious" of its own inner dichotomy. It seems to be do so through the simultaneous deployment of at least two different perspectives: one within, and one outside the Self. This is the only way through which to distinguish and thus to place in opposition two antithetical aspects, which here are the poles of the dyad of good and evil. This brings about a transformation in the ways in which the archetype expresses itself in psychic reality, even to the final extreme of finding incarnation in its own creature. This would also seem to be the source of the seductive but far from immediately clear positions which Jung assumes with respect to a number of exceptional "biographies," which from this point of view can be seen to represent a self-realization of the unconscious.

The pursuit of such an hypothesis also means that we must consider the possibility that an archetype can assume a "consciousness" of its own. This transformation, moreover, would be effected by simply "being conscious" of the consciousness of the Ego, which in turn would become an element with the power to transform the archetype. In other words, in addition to being an extension of the Self, the Ego would first of all rank as a functional extension through which the Self is able to grow conscious of itself. And this, I believe, might be the final goal of the process of individuation.

I would also like to underline the importance of the act of representation, and as well of its functions of transformation. The creature is potentially capable of modifying its creator by making the creator "see" what in fact he is "doing" to his creature, or by giving those actions "visibility." Thus, God, the Creator, was able to direct his "destructive fury" at Job, his creature, for the purpose of effecting the realization of the ethic of life which He himself had planned. In other words, the analyst ought to be able to provide the patient with valid tools with which to activate a "different" space where conditions can be so arranged as to allow the unrepresentable to become representable. And no matter if the space in which representation occurs is the space of dream, or a situation, as in sandplay therapy, in which the analyst intervenes to furnish patients with particular tools for the stimulation of their capacities of representation, the final result is the same: *the subject learns to perceive himself/herself in objective terms,* and thus to exist at one and the very same time both as Self and as Other than Self. Jung's words thus assume a special importance for the moments – such as in dream, or during the creation of a sandbox image – in which I take on the twofold role of *both* creator and creature. But still there's a choice to be made: 1) I am free to do nothing and can thereby submit to the self-complacency of my subjectivity that creates and destroys with no understanding of the ethics of either the one or the other; or 2) I can seize the opportunity to lay the bases of a broader awareness which can activate processes of transformation.

These brief reflections on "Answer to Job" can perhaps be best fleshed out by looking at a clinical case, since the images produced by sandplay are highly complex phenomena. This is all the more clear when patients view slides of their sandbox constructions of previous years or months and discover their recollections of their images to be in fact quite different, either partially or wholly, from what they actually created; they may even voice disavowal of images which they themselves had made. It's useful to remember the degree to which a sandbox construction can be a harbinger of a patient's coming to awareness of his/her own internal objects and psychic dynamics; this has led me indeed to a profound realization of how often I myself have "failed to remember" or perhaps have "deformed" the original object which a patient produced. Such deformations are a times a question of shifting the images set up in the sandbox, but at others are episodes of true and proper blindness.

Carla is a patient who was referred to me a colleague.

She is forty years old, married, and has one child. She works in the field of mental health, and her job entails a high degree of responsibility. She decided to enter analysis after beginning to suffer from panic attacks, accompanied by shifts in mood. From the time of our very first sessions, I noted the presence of borderline qualities in Carla's personality, as revealed by a complex of persecution which on the one hand activated attacks of panic, while leading on the other to alternating periods of absolute inertia.

We agreed to meet twice a week.

Figure 1

Carla made her first sandplay construction in the course of her second session. She selected only two figures: a singing Chinese woman and a small crate of fish. The crate of fish seemed at first to refer to the space of the sandbox itself. But these two figures with so many possible ways of relating to one another in any case proved to be very useful within the analytical process. In commenting on the image she had made in the sand, Carla herself remarked that the crate of fish reminded her of a recent dream in which her father seemed to "sow" fish eggs in the sea: "Who knows," she asked, "if one of the newborn fish will manage to reach the woman?" I recall quite clearly that during this session I experienced an ill-defined feeling of discomfort with respect to this crate of fish (which in reality were made of grains of rice, painted gray and glued together).

In the following sessions, sandbox work was again employed as a tool of the patient's analysis, but I had repressed that indefinable but urgent feeling I had felt. Carla was then abruptly to discontinue her analysis, in a sudden and extreme episode of acting out, and I myself experienced this event as a painful combination of frustration, failure and relief. Only later was I able to return to an analysis of the patient's work, and what follows is a brief account of its most significant moments.

First of all, it's best to go back to my immediate awareness of the importance of Carla's first sand construction (especially in relation to the first dreams she brought to analysis) and as well to the sense of vague discomfort it provoked in me. Both need to be dealt with. In my revisitation of Carla's analysis, that sensation proved to be fundamental.

By choosing the crate of fish, Carla from the very beginning had signaled her dimension of "adhesive identification," which in fact connected with a psychic two-dimensionality in which no "third" dimension could find adequate room for expression. Separation could only be radical and sudden.

Some time after analysis had been interrupted, I managed to interpret a dream that Carla had presented immediately following that first sand construction, and it brought me to the realization that I had been unable to "think through" the messages which the patient deliberately had sent me from the beginning.

In the dream, she is in a park, where she picks up a wounded bird (a goldfinch) and then sees three small elephants "one on top of the other ... it looked like they had fallen and gotten stuck to one other." Carla's associations allowed me to link the goldfinch with her father – it referred to a number of episodes in which her father and these birds were the main characters – but the elephants remained an enigma for both of us. Now, however, in retrospect, it is clear that Carla's dream was a courageous reformulation of her sand construction: the wounded goldfinch, of which she remembered the singing, referred to the singing Chinese woman, whereas the three gray elephants stuck together "one on top of the other" referred directly to the gray-painted rice-grain fish glued together in the crate. Carla, in fact, had provided herself (and me) with a great deal of information: that singing Chinese woman had to be "thought of" as wounded, and one had to understand those fish to be as heavy as elephants. And, finally, Carla's work with the sandbox had signaled the extent to which her "three" or "third" was stuck and adherent: the bond was so strong as to allow her to express herself only in terms of "two."

I might have intervened by pointing out the similarity between the fish in the sandbox and the small elephants in the dream. Such an interpretation would have linked a number of elements that Carla had brought to the analysis: the representation she had arranged in the sandbox, the dream that derived from it, and the dynamics of transference which already had emerged so forcefully when Carla had said to me: "Have I been too heavy? I'm afraid that I am too heavy. I'd like you to hold me in your arms."

I had failed to give adequate consideration to the fact that the patient's image in the sandbox had also constellated my countertransference. In other words, the "creature" that consisted of the sandbox had modified not only the "creator" that consisted of the patient, but as well that other "creator" that consisted of the *partners* in the analytical dyad. This failure in fact had led me to overlook the "heaviness," the sense of oppression, and as well the destructiveness transmitted by those fish all "glued together." In reality, the patient's work in the sandbox had given me the opportunity to activate an analytical situation which would have been able right from start to accept and elaborate that two-dimensional destructiveness with which she so impellingly felt herself to be afflicted. The loss of the possibility to accept and elaborate it was destined to lead the analysis, as in fact took place, to succumb to it.

The next two constructions that Carla created in the sandbox were very similar to one another, at one and then four weeks distance from the first construction. A number of objects were used in both, and placed in the same positions. These sandbox images were "activated" by Carla's hands, and marked by the presence of persons and objects which need not here be described in detail. It's of interest, however, to direct attention to some of the comments she made while working on them.

After constructing a mountain she remarked: "I'd like some sky to show ..." (she set to uncovering a bit of the blue bottom of the sandbox) ... "but it's hard to get it separated out."

"It needs some people" (she put in two separate child figurines, but placed them one next to the other). "But this isn't what I mean.... These two are a little bit fused together."

She laid down a small aluminum rod that branches in two at one end, saying: "something that forks from a single whole."

In the course of this month of work with Carla, I encountered a number of the typical features of the borderline personality, which Carla showed me "in her own way." Carla was confined to a two-dimensional emotional life by the dramatically "crippled" presence of a third dimension which was incapable of symbolization, and which thereby prevented her from elaborating relationships, whether internally or externally.

"I need to get close to things in order to push them away. That's even a physical sensation."

The sandbox construction where the division or horizon line was dug out at the foot of the mountain provides a tangible sign of this situation. It was only later, on looking at the photo of the scene, that I also saw the horizon, and only then did I realize that Carla's constructions in the sandbox were only in appearance three-dimensional; in reality, they were dramatically "flat" and two-dimensional.... It was only when looking at photos of Carla's creations that I managed to see the horizon that so dramatically oppressed her.

Her aggressiveness toward the father-phallus-breast-analyst came out all at once. The attacks directed against her father, who suffered from cancer, dramatically overlapped with those against her mother, whom she described as a selfish woman who, given the father's effective absence, assumed the role of imposing "rules and limits," striking out violently at Carla whenever she did anything wrong, and withholding all expression of affection or solidarity. I alternately experienced myself as a breast from which Carla would have liked to be nursed and, at much the same time, as a phallus that she wanted to castrate, criticizing my interpretations and my capacity for clear thought.

This was the situation in which the fourth of the series of sandbox constructions precipitated, seven months after the third. And here we'll find it useful to describe the construction in detail.

She began the session by saying that she was reading a book by Mhasud Khan, and that she had very much been struck by a phrase about "mixtures of the life and death instincts." She found herself thinking, as though surprised at her ignorance, that she had never learned the art of mixing and kneading bread or pastry dough, and she then continued that she thought of these two instincts as separate things that had to run parallel to one another, and which never ought to be blended, mixed, intertwined or confused with each other.

She then stood up and went to the sandbox. She poured some water into it, gathered together the wet sand and began to mix it. While doing so, she remarked: "Let's imagine that we're mixing this together with ... in any case, I feel angry ... here it doesn't bother me to get my hands dirty, but it does when I have to do something with flour at home ... it sticks to my hands and I can't stand that. I think that whenever I start to knead flour I feel an energy that enters my hands, and that's something I just can't stand ... (she adds more water to the sand and continues mixing it) ... I think about strangling my father ... like this! (she forcefully squeezes the mixture) ... I am very angry, it makes me grit my teeth ..."

At this point Carla hunched over, and I saw a shiver run through her body ... she sighed and held herself still. She kept her hands immersed in the mixture of sand and water in the sandbox. She began to breathe deeply, as though catching air with difficulty. She said: "Do you know what I feel? I feel that my fingers ... I feel my tongue, as though I wanted ... to suck, to suck on something but not to drink milk ... perhaps that's the reason my hands and legs sometimes go paralyzed ... but why? ... anyway, I feel all the strength I have. I don't understand why I'm squeezing so hard, or what am I squeezing. I have an unbelievable need to be doing this!" (by now, for quite some time, she was no longer mixing the sand, but was rhythmically squeezing her hands in the mixture she had already made) ... "maybe I find a pleasure in feeling so much strength, so much energy ... I could make some sort of construction here, but I feel right now that ... no! Now, I don't feel like constructing anything, I just like the feel of this thing, just the way it is!"

She stopped moving her hands in the wet sand and removed them from the sandbox. Time had run out, and the session was over. Carla took her leave rather hastily, leaving me alone with … what?

I remained there alone in the room with a pile of sand. In the course of the session I had felt that my stomach was being split open, I could not catch my breath, or find the voice with which to ask her to stop, to go no further in her strangling, her tender caressing, her sucking. … I had felt myself to be father and mother and pure, unadulterated flesh.

I remained there looking at the mound of wet sand, and thought that for now a pile of sand was all I'd be able to see. I was also thinking that Carla had delivered a powerful blow, if, with all she had said and done, I couldn't come up with any sort of image or with even a snatch of a thought. I felt relieved that the session was over, but I also felt I'd find it hard to recover my ability to think things through where Carla was concerned.

Events began to move at a quickened pace. Carla's father suddenly worsened, and he died within three months. A few sessions later, Carla dreamt of me lying on a cot: blood flowed from my mouth, and I gave her a sign that I was dying.

Two developments in the analytical relationship seem noteworthy: my interpretations became more incisive; and I realized I had begun to manage, for the first time, to find the "proper distance" I had to maintain with Carla, and "correctly" to elaborate the psychic materials and the dynamics of the transfer.

Carla made three more sandbox images, but her way of using the sandbox was here entirely different: she turned the sandbox into a sort of blackboard on which she used her fingers to trace out diagrams or sketches of dreams that she felt unable to describe in any other adequate way.

In the first she drew a rectangle with three dots at its sides. She told me she had dreamt of a dinner table where she, her father and her mother had all been seated, but she couldn't remember exactly where her mother had been: the rectangle was the table; she herself was the dot on its upper long side; her father sat at the head of the table; ... her mother ... here! ... directly facing her (and she marked the point with the imprint of her index finger).

In the second sandbox image she drew a small spiral, and she told me of having dreamt that she couldn't find her son. Then she had seen a hole in ground; she leaned out over it and saw that it disappeared into the depths, its walls "covered over with the bodies of boys" who seemed as though to be swept away by a swirling current that pulled them ever further downward. She saw her son among them, stretched out her hand to him, and succeeded in pulling him out.

Figure 2

In the third and last of these sandbox images, Carla drew what appeared to be two triangles touching at their vertices. She told me that this image had entered her mind while she was waking up: two crossed blades.

Figure 3

During the month that followed her father's death, Carla's husband told her he had been having an affair with another woman. In the week after that, Carla phoned to let me know that she had moved back to the town where she had been born. "I'm sorry not to have told you anything about it.... I did it all in just two days."

The analysis had been broken off.

Conclusions

The last three sandbox images that Carla made before discontinuing analysis bear a few more words of discussion. Though my first reaction to these "graphic" images was marked by a feeling of distress – so much so that I neglected to photograph the first of them – other considerations were later to come into play.

Carla was depositing her dreams in the sandbox, as though she had found a container for the inner reality to which she had never before had access. I believe that having "contained" both Carla and myself in the sandbox with the "mixture" of sand and water allowed my body to live and think its way through a multitude of dynamics of transference-countertransference, projective identifications and counter-identifications that allowed me to move more suitably among the various dimensions of transference that Carla had set in motion. This allowed me, in turn, to furnish interpretations and various other interventions which she found to be helpful and not confusing, since they were suited to the kind of transference that was underway.

I have come to feel that these last three sandbox images – within a process that experienced a great and sudden acceleration – testify to my presence as a "third" which was just sufficiently efficacious to allow Carla to begin to make use of an interior space in which to hold her inner reality. That space, for the moment, was represented by the sandbox-blackboard which served not only as a container, but as a tool through which to make or allow me to see.

Considering the pathological dimension of fusional relationship with which Carla entered analysis, this act of allowing me to see, or of "showing" me, also expressed her achievement of an awareness of an Other than Self.

The End?

Seven years have now gone by.
The telephone rings.
I recognize the voice at once.
Carla.
She tells me that she did not really move to another city ... but the events which she had been going through had in every way been more than she could take. "I feel the need to thank you ... in these last few years I have changed a lot ... maybe it sounds absurd, but it's still too early and I'd like to ask if later on I can call you again, so that we can set up another appointment..."

This conversation now took place two years ago.

References

1 Jung, C. G. (1952), "Answer to Job," in *Collected Works*, Vol. 2, pp. 355-470, 1958, 2nd edition 1969, London: Routledge & Kegan Paul.
2 Ibid., p. 42.

On Resonance

Ruth Ammann

This paper is an attempt to sum up my reflections on the phenomenon of resonance, a subject that has preoccupied me for many years.

When I was working as an architect, I asked myself: "What happens between my client and me when we plan their home together? Is our collaboration one of a good, helpful resonance or of dissonance?

Then again, what happens to us when we visit a foreign city? Do we feel well, because the beauty and carefully elaborated architecture resonates positively with our senses and feelings? Or, do we feel physically and psychically miserable, because the buildings emanate gray, cold carelessness and sheer routine or profit thinking?

I have written about these interesting questions in several other publications[1], but I have not yet written about an important "architectural" aspect which is related to my work – in fact to the work of all of us as analysts or psychotherapists: "How do our practice rooms influence our client's therapeutic process? Is it a place of good resonance, good in the sense of helpful for the therapy? Or a negative one? How do our clients react to these very fine vibrations in a room? Or we could also ask: how does the emanation of the room interact with our clients?"

Up to now I rarely heard a colleague speak about the practice room as an important factor of the therapeutic setting. Maybe one does not notice its influence on other people, as long one works in one's own room and is in harmony with it!

I became conscious of this aspect when I had the opportunity to work in other colleagues' practice rooms, especially in other sandplay therapists' sandplay rooms. In some cases I felt at ease in their rooms, in others I was very irritated by the lack of a suitable ambiance of their space or the lack of – for me – important figures such as religious figures, ugly, not perfectly aesthetic objects or material that still can be shaped. This "not being in a good resonance" with the working space, then clearly manifested itself in my work. I was not in harmony with that room, I was not balanced.

We say: "I feel well or do not feel well in my skin," and everybody understands the meaning of that saying. Yet the room in which we work is so to speak our third skin (the second one would be our clothing). Therefore it is obvious that we should feel well also in our third skin.

In this way, through working in other analysts' rooms, I have experienced for myself what a client must sense when he or she is in a positive or a negative resonance with the analyst's room. The interaction between an analysand and his or her analysts working room is definitely an important constellating aspect of the analytical work.

Another field where vibrations, or to put it better, waves play a great role, is the world of colors. When I work with colors in general, with art, with colors in architecture or with the therapeutic paintings of my clients, I am very much aware that colors are waves and each color transfers a specific energy to us. We enter into different resonance with the energy field of each different color. In therapy even the color of our clothing can be important.[2]

Or, in the garden, which is my and many other people's favorite living space, the phenomenon of resonance is also very much alive. We experience the fascinating and healing effect of gardens or gardening, because in the garden we are in resonance with the forces and infinite wisdom of Nature. We are embedded in the rhythm of morning and evening, the eternally returning, great cycles of the seasons – we are in harmony or in disharmony with the surrounding Nature. Jung expresses this state of being beautifully in his book, *Memories, Dreams, Reflections*. There he says about his life at the Tower in Bollingen: "In Bollingen I am in modest harmony with Nature."[3]

We all know how meaningful the interaction between humans and vegetation is, be it with trees, plants or flowers. We experience this in the garden, the fields, the woods. Yet already on a very small scale we sense the healthy, positive emanation of plants. If one has green plants or – what is even more effective – freshly cut flowers in a room, the whole room immediately begins to resonate, it becomes alive. Interesting was the remark of a client, when one day I had no flowers in my room. She asked me whether I was sick. I was surprised and asked her why she thought so. "You have no flowers in your room," she answered.

Because of all these experiences, I began to formulate my questions about the resonance of sounds, rooms, colors, Nature and other things in our environment. These questions became the stepping stones to lead me towards the most important question: "What happens between me and my client during a verbal analysis or a so-called nonverbal sandplay therapy, in which one indeed speaks less, but senses more? Which energies are at work in a therapeutic session? And where begins and ends the so-called interactive or therapeutic field?" Specifically I began to reflect on the following: "What else happens *above and beyond* the effective and intelligent use of the Jungian psychotherapeutic technique? What else – other than mutual projections, elements of transference and counter-transference – may determine the effectiveness of a therapy?" I also want to know: "What is it really that makes my work as an analyst successful and unique?" I want to know this, because I am convinced that, if there is nothing unique in my work I would prefer to have another job.

The formulation of my questions may be seen as narcissistic, but it is not so.

My concern grows out of the experiences of many years of psychotherapeutic work and the observation that our profession comes more and more under the pressure of factors such as "efficiency, economy, time pressure etc." Many of my colleagues and I are very concerned that more and more the concept of psychotherapy seems to be seen as a technique with the goal of making people function – function like well-functioning machines. Of course we *do not deny* that a person must "function" in order to survive in our world. And we *do not neglect* the clinical, psychiatric components of psychotherapy. But still we see the meaning of psychotherapy in a larger and deeper way: It means to help a person towards healing and developing his or her own personality. The Jungian term "individuation" does not just mean to be able to function well in the world: it also means developing and unfolding the uniqueness of one's talents and potential and finally using them for the community with our fellow human beings. Psychotherapy, be it a Jungian analysis or Jungian sandplay therapy, is far more than "a technique." I would like to show what I mean by "far more than a technique" with an example from music, probably the best-known field of resonance:

A great musician is not the one with a perfect technique, but the one who is able to move people's hearts, to create a resonance between his way of making music alive for himself and the audience. We all know the story of Orpheus, the greatest singer and musician of "all" times. He could even move stones with his music. Not with his technique, but with his music he transferred the vibrations of his heart to the stone's "heart." To move a stone – and to move a human soul – is an art and a mystery, not a technique.

Fortunately, opposed to the growing and harassing tendency of seeing psychotherapy predominantly as a short, economic, efficient technique, there is both new and old research on the question: "What is really effective in therapy?"

Reading in Peter Hain's book, *Das Geheimnis therapeutischer Wirkung*,[4] the interviews with many great, successful and well-known psychotherapists, such as Frank Farrelly, Siegfried Mrochen, Paul Watzlawick, Helm Stierlin, Cloé Madanes and others on the topic: "What is effective in our psychotherapeutic work?", we can sum up their opinions as follows: It is not, or not first of all, the technique or the principle of a specific school (Jungian, Freudian, etc.), nor the right use of medications that work in therapy, but the most meaningful factor is the personality of the therapist. Most of them mentioned values such as "authenticity, optimism, integrity, honesty and creativity," and what we Jungians might add is "the capacity to encourage and activate the self-healing capacity of the psyche."

In addition, they mentioned as specifically important: curiosity, humor, intuition and the capacity to observe precisely (which of course is especially important for sandplay therapists!).

So what is important: To learn the craft of psychotherapy or to develop and refine in a holistic way one's own personality? Or both? Certainly it's both: an excellent training in psychotherapy and a refinement of the personality are both needed. For this – the refinement of the personality – we know in German an especially fine and apt expression: we speak of "Bildung des Herzens," the "education of the heart," which my dictionary translates as "cultivation of the moral faculties." Yet this translation is not quite correct. In the German meaning of the "education of the heart" there is much more to that expression. The "heart" is an unfathomable and mysterious symbol. It is tightly connected with "love," "Eros" and "relatedness." Therefore one must add "love," "Eros" and "relatedness" to the already mentioned qualities that are effective in therapy.

Thus let us return to the phenomenon of resonance. Speaking of hearts, I want to show a picture.

It's the last sand picture of a client of mine, a young woman 38 years old. She was in her sixth year of analysis-sandplay therapy with me, because she suffered from an hereditary progressive muscular dystrophy. For about four years she rarely talked about this very serious disease – it was too painful for her. On the contrary, she talked about different problems, which were certainly also important, but, in the light of her severe illness, rather secondary. Her drawings and her sand pictures, however, always spoke another language, namely, the language of the body, of a suffering body.

Picture 1

I was always conscious that, because of the progressive nature of her illness, there was no real cure for her body. But within myself, I held up the hope that her soul could be healed through a reconciliation with her suffering body.

And indeed slowly, very slowly this reconciliation happened. During the last year of therapy she created in each session a sand picture. Through shaping a positive image in the sand, she said, she could balance the pain of knowing how ill her body was.

One morning – it was one of those mild and sunny Spring days – she went to the sand tray and created this sand picture.

She explained the picture in this way: "The two elephants are you and me. The small elephant is finally in resonance with the big one." While she was saying this, she held the monkey in her hands. This monkey had represented in many previous sand pictures her weak and "inferior" body. Now she massaged his hands and feet, as if she wanted to warm them up. Then she put him down into the field of "resonance," the heart-shaped blue space in the center of the tray.

What did she mean by saying: "The small elephant is in resonance with the big one" or in other words: "Finally I am in resonance with you"? What kind of a resonance, did she feel? And what was its origin and what was its consequence?

For the answer let us pause a moment, because the answer may become more evident once we have understood the meaning of "resonance."

The phenomenon of resonance is mainly known in connection with music. Its principle is simple, but powerful. If one touches a key on the piano, soon the octave, the fifth and the third begin vibrating, and then the whole piano resonates.

Or, if you have in your hands a violin with four strings and another violin with four strings lying on a table beside you, the strings on the violin on the table will start to vibrate as soon as you start to play your violin.

If you are a poor violinist and you have a violin with only one string, then only one string of the violin on the table will start to move. But if you have a wonderful instrument with ten strings, then not only will the violin on the table pick up all the vibrations, but perhaps other instruments in the room will start to quiver.

I know that this example of the poor or the wonderfully rich violin is not quite correct, but it is an excellent metaphor for how resonance interplays and acts between human beings. If an analyst is a "poor instrument," he or she will not be able to bring to life the analysand's instrument. On the other hand, an analyst with a very "differentiated instrument with many strings," which means an analyst with a very differentiated, rich personality, will have enormous difficulties to awaken or build up a sleeping or not yet existing string in his or her analysand.

Certainly it is not so that analyst and analysand are always in a well-balanced resonance or harmony. Rather the opposite is true. Analyst and analysand transfer in the beginning of a therapy different vibrations. However the predominant waves, such as love, Eros and trust in life which are necessary for the development of psyche and body must come from the analyst's side. That is what my analysand at this moment (after six years) showed in her picture, because right from the beginning of her therapeutic process she used the big elephant as a symbol for life energy, authenticity and a caring relationship. The fact, however, that she connected the qualities of the big elephant with me, she told me explicitly only at the moment when she shaped this last sand picture.

For now, let us return to exploring the principle of "resonance."

From the example of the piano, we understand that the principle of resonance creates a wholeness, a harmony of sounds, tones and overtones. This is not only the case in music or acoustics.

Here, I would like to quote some thoughts from Friedrich Cramer's work. Professor Cramer was born in 1923, has a doctorate in natural sciences and was from 1962-1991 Director of the Max Planck Institute for experimental medicine in Göttingen, Germany. In his book, *Symphony des Lebendigen* [Symphony of the Living Things][5], Cramer writes that resonance renders wholeness possible in all vibrating systems such as: atoms, molecules, the human brain, evolution, and so many others. He defines "resonance" as the element that holds the world together in its innermost essence (*im Innersten*) and that creates all interactions between body and mind, between one person and another, between an individual and society etc. All these interactions can be seen as mutually attuned vibrations. Resonance means always that vibrations interact, modify and overlay each other. In doing so, they can stimulate and intensify each other or diminish and extinguish each other.

A vibration or undulation needs a medium, such as water for waves in the sea, air for the sound, the electromagnetic field for the light, the earth for earthquakes or the sand in the sandplay therapy for expressing bodily sensations and their emotions. Furthermore, there are all the manifold physical, emotional and spiritual vibrations weaving back and forth between two persons, creating what we can call a therapeutic resonance field.

Resonance transfers energy, it effects and causes movement and changes. Therefore, because resonance is a form of transferring energy, it is very important for us to be most heedful and sensitive to the manifold vibrations that touch us or go out from us. We as humans can transfer life-enhancing, constructive energies or we can emanate life-hindering, destructive energies. For our health's sake and for other people's sake we must therefore be careful not to pick up and not to send out negative, destructive energies.

As in this paper I don't have the possibility to offer more amplifying examples of resonance, I invite the readers to ponder for a while the phenomenon of resonance in their own daily lives and in their therapeutic work. I invite them to consider the influence of their own personal conditions, of their therapy rooms and settings, of the seasons and the weather outside the therapy room, the prevailing political situation and other elements of daily life that may determine a therapeutic session.

Now, let us return to the analysand who suffers from progressive muscular dystrophy. I call her Pia.

Picture 1, with the two elephants joining each other "in resonance," as Pia said, was the last picture she made. I now want to go back in time over six years and show two drawings from the very beginning of her analysis (Pictures 2 and 3) and then show a few significant sand pictures from the series of over 70 trays she did over these years. She came to see me every two weeks for a 1 1/2 hours long session, with quite long interruptions from time to time because of her or my vacations.

Picture 2

Certainly one is at first shocked by this human figure, which looks horrified and numbed. The blue color reinforces the impression of the body being frozen – frozen with fright. Lots of little knives are stabbing the body, and sweat is dripping down. It was cold sweat that Pia produced as soon as the suffering and imperfection of her body was – even just minimally – touched. And of course, in resonance with her ill and imperfect body, she always devalued her whole personality. This "cold sweating" was an enormous problem for her.

In the beginning of the therapy she was not conscious of the origin of her fear and cold sweating. At this time her real trauma was still hidden. Yet every time the trauma was even minimally and unconsciously touched, she started to freeze and sweat at the same time. So the picture first of all expresses a terrified body, frozen in horror and pain.

Yet, if one looks carefully, two other elements can be recognized: Lots of round yellow elements with friendly faces are visible, and the foot in the lower left corner is shaped like a leaf.

This leaf-shaped foot seemed to me like a promising possibility of getting helpful and nourishing energy from a natural element. This one foot looked as if it were rooted in Mother Nature.

The yellow faces appeared to me friendly and protective – in any case, very different from the horrified blue figure in the center of the picture. I saw them as light, positive cells, which hold together the blue figure that seems to explode or dissociate. Right from the beginning I had the fantasy that these luminous elements had something to do with Pia's immune system. It was there, but "looking away" and not strong enough to help the horrified body.

My client, however, did not notice the friendly, yellow faces. Even though I gently tried to call her attention to them, she was not able to see them, because she was totally focused on the disastrous, pathological side of her life. So at this moment of the beginning of her therapy, she was unconsciously drawing helpful elements, but she was not able to see or accept and use them as positive resources.

What was there to do? From my experience, I know that the psyche works slowly, it takes its time, it cannot be pushed. Especially severely traumatized persons are extremely sensitive and vulnerable. Therefore, at this moment it would not have been helpful to insist by alluding to the helpful aspects in her own drawing. She could not have received the message. Thus I trusted the healing effect of playing and I suggested to her to do sandplay.

Playing – what has playing to do with resonance, and why is there a chance for development and healing in playful activities?

Playing consists in the creative resonance between the fixed structure of the given rules and the flexible openness of the outcome. In sandplay, the rules are given in the time and space of the setting and by the limitations of the sand and objects, the figures or miniatures. The result, however, of the playful interaction between the analysand and sand, water and figures or the outcome of the mutually resonating influences between the analysand and the analyst, are totally open. Conscious and unconscious elements, aspects of feeling and of reason interact. Spiritual and concrete physical aspects are intertwined. Vibrations of the analyst and of the analysand resonate, which means that a mutual bodily resonance, a feeling resonance and an intellectual or spiritual resonance becomes awakened. In this field of activated resonances, there is always the possibility of a new creative turn or twist. If a person is really playing, the result of the play is not preconceived – on the contrary, surprising changes take birth.

These components of true playing offer the chance for changes in a client's psychic patterns or in his view of himself, his fellow humans and the world. These changes don't happen in one or two weeks, but during each session of sandplay, play after play, rigid, frozen structures get broken up, and inner and outer values are slowly transformed and renewed. An inner, mainly unconscious wisdom – which in Jungian terminology is called the Self – is guiding the process of healing and renewal. We can trust it. There is the tendency of self-healing in us, but we must give it the possibility to become alive and manifest itself. In this therapeutic method of sandplay, the secret of healing is hidden in creative play!

Let us return to the therapeutic process of my client. Before she began to do sandplay, she made another drawing.

Picture 3

Here, we see a horrible face with hands reaching out and stabbing a little, obviously intimidated human being. Pia saw in this big, dominating face all the negative, swallowing aspects of the outer world which were against her, including her grandfather and mother from whom she had inherited her disease. She felt disvalued by her father and other people because of her ill body and also humiliated because she could not be a mother, although she was married and loved children very much. She identified with the shy little person in the left lower corner and experienced herself as tortured, wounded and devalued

254

by "the overwhelmingly aggressive others." She said, that the discrepancy between the terribly menacing outer world and the vulnerability of herself, created an "ice cold" depression in her, represented in this drawing by the black line with blue icicles.

At the beginning of our work together, she saw all the negative elements destroying her as outside of herself. Some years later, she could also see this threatening face in the drawing as her own face. As much as she became able to acknowledge her positive inner resources, she could also accept her own self-destructive sides.

Picture 4

After three months of therapy, Pia did the above sand picture (her ninth sand picture, not the initial picture). Interestingly, the motif of the icicles and the black line reappeared. Both are made with paper, which makes the sand picture look like a drawing. Under the black line we see a little turquoise hippopotamus, a figure that Pia loved and often used for herself.

On the black line, in the center of the tray, there lies a figure, which Pia called "The negative element." So we see that the ice and the depression are still there. The little Hippo is still under the ice cold depression. But from the right, upper corner, the big elephant comes in and touches the ice with its trunk. At the time Pia did the tray, she only mentioned that the elephant 'fertilized' the ice and warmed it up. But let us remember that Pia saw the elephant right from the beginning as a symbol for life energy, authenticity and positive relationship. Let us also recall that in explaining the "Resonance Picture" (Picture 1), done after six years of therapy, Pia clearly connected the big elephant with me. So retrospectively, we might say that I (or the whole therapeutic setting!) obviously radiated a life-giving, warming energy, which began to melt the ice.

Picture 5

After another two months, Pia shaped this picture, which again looks more like a drawing. Pia does not touch the sand:

she is creating a mixture between a drawing, a collage and a sand picture. The icicles are still there and the little Hippo is still in a black cage. But in the top of the tray we notice a sun which is melting the ice or the sweat, represented by drops which under the black line become red and finally form as if a red line or lake on the lower edge of the tray. From then on, red elements always represented warmth and life.

In the upper left corner we see some silver snakes moving from the direction where I was sitting towards the sun. We can easily empathize with what Pia later timidly said, namely that good energy was moving from my side to the warming sun – and as if she wanted to thank me for that good energy, she then put a red heart in the sand with two little gift parcels on it. She smiled again and murmured: "One is for you." The other parcel was obviously for herself.

Here we observe for the first time the motive of the heart as a positive, warm field containing two objects, one belonging to Pia and one to me. I was very moved by this picture, and I asked myself how I had merited this gift. What had I done, said, felt or unconsciously expressed? Looking back after many years, I believe that it was nothing specific, but rather a broad stream of warmth and esteem that I felt for that vulnerable, lovely young woman. I did not feel especially sorry for her because of her illness, since I saw very realistically that there was no real physical cure for her. Much more importantly, I saw her delicate, wounded soul and her anxious but very creative spirit. And – as was said before – I continued to hope that her soul and spirit could be healed through a reconciliation with her suffering body.

Pia went on creating sand pictures. After another seven months, she shaped Picture 6.

Picture 6

Here we see the big elephant in the center, lying in a red (wooden) leaf. The elephant is surrounded by red (warm, lively!) balls, and the little silver snakes show that energy is radiating outward from that center. Already in the last picture the elephant was lying in or held and contained by this leaf, which again reminded me of the leaf-shaped foot in Pia's first drawing. I interpreted that leaf in this way, that the positive life energy, symbolized by the elephant, was itself carried by Nature, by the healing force of Nature in Pia, in myself and in the powerful Nature surrounding my house and practice room. Indeed, I am convinced that the view from my practice room over the garden, the woods and hills is very peaceful, comforting and healing.

Then, Pia took the little Hippo, put it in a nest of orange-colored paper and placed it in the upper right corner. Again, this arrangement looks like an anticipation of the picture of "Resonance" (Picture I), because in resonance with the power-ful healing energy of the elephant, the little Hippo can come out of the black jail of depression, whereupon it gets a little nest of orange paper – orange being the color of returning life[6].

After this sand picture, Pia created many sand pictures during two years, and we had intense dialogues about her personal or matrimonial and her professional problems. The sand pictures still had more the character of drawings. Pia hardly touched the sand, but covered it with an abundance of objects, clearly showing a resistance to go deeper into her physical problem. She was still very shy, vulnerable and had great difficulties showing her feelings of joy or to cry.

After about three years of therapy, I felt that our therapeutic relationship was now strong and stable enough to allow me to take a step forward. During the next session, I said to Pia that I had observed her hesitation to go deeper into the sand and that I felt that she could now try it. Pia was not shocked nor blocked. She simply touched the ground, i.e., she dug down to the bottom of the tray. This moment was a real turning point. Pia now started to shape many different images representing her body in the sand.

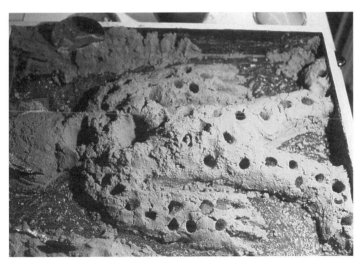

Picture 7

259

Some of them, like the one in Picture 7, she perforated violently in order to show me how violated and perforated she felt and how painfully she experienced her body. She told me that it felt as if there were holes in her muscles and that she sensed the growing weakness of her body.

This period in her analysis was in a specific way very painful also for me. My analysand transferred her emotions, such as pain, desperation and fear in very violent movements to the sand. What she felt within, she acted out with her hands in the sand. I was sitting quite near her and watched attentively what happened. In those moments, her powerful emotions and actions created a very strong body resonance between her and myself. I was deeply touched by her emotions which she acted out, and I sensed her pain in my own body.

This was not a unique experience for me. I think that most sandplay therapists know the sensations and emotions which that body resonance creates, be it a gentle, caressing or a violent, hurting one. If we as analysts are physically and emotionally really present, we cannot and should not avoid being moved, or sometimes even shaken, by our analysands' life expressions – otherwise we would not be authentic. That is why the analytical work with this material medium "sand" goes more "under the skin" than verbal analysis. This is also why a sandplay therapist after the session not only must reflect on what happened, but also needs to let go of the emotional and physical influences that he or she picked up from the analysand. Maybe the simple, hands-on activities like taking a photo of the sand picture, cleaning the tray and smoothing the sand are excellent parts of a self-cleansing ritual.

Picture 8

After some weeks Pia shaped this interesting sand picture. We see a hill or a mollusk or, in retrospect, we might see it as a body cell. Life in the form of small turtles is growing out of it, and out of the center powerfully rises the big elephant, which as we know, represented for Pia *the* basic life energy, warmth and trust. This picture was the beginning of many representations of cellular structures. I noticed very soon what she was shaping, and later on also Pia became dimly aware of what she was doing. Unconsciously, and later subconsciously, she began to deal with her profoundest problem, the muscular dystrophy. As we see in Picture 9, one of many examples, she imagined the cells, those very small, but ill parts of her body and started to give them life enhancing objects.

During the many years of working as a sandplay therapist, I have seen many organic forms in the sand, but never before someone had gone so deeply and consistently into the somatic part of her problem.

261

Picture 9

Here, Pia's psyche started to take care of her body. In many sand pictures (all of which I cannot show here), she imagined her cells in the sand and warmed them with suns and a little oil lamp. Again and again she nourished them with red glass stones, fruits and vegetables. She now talked a lot about her disease both with me and with her doctor.

After more than a year, she formed Picture 10.

On a central circle, we see the monkey whom Pia had used in many previous sand pictures as a symbol for her suffering body. Here, the monkey is spread out and exposed to the world, but at the same time protected and surrounded by a sun like circle. On this circle we notice red (warm, positive!) glass drops. Furthermore, we see a great number of smurfs [dwarf figures from a popular cartoon], all looking at the monkey and – as Pia commented – bringing good energies and lovely gifts. She said that the smurfs represented positive, protecting elements bringing healing and joy to the monkey – to her body.

Picture 10

Immediately, when Pia expressed this, I recalled the yellow faces in her first drawing (Picture 2), which surrounded the horrified, frozen blue person, the self-image of Pia. After the many years we had worked together, I thought that the time had come to point to the connection between that first drawing and the actual sand picture. Pia smiled and agreed with me. She said that she now felt ready to acknowledge and accept helping energy from within herself and from without, something she had not been able to do at the time when she did the drawing. We had a long discussion about the possibility or the choice we have in our life to accept and sustain and even to build up our immune system, which means to physically and psychically care for ourselves, or else to neglect, deny and destroy our self-healing forces, and together with these, also ourselves.

A few sessions later, Pia shaped the following sand picture.

Picture 11

Again we see a cell-like structure, on which smurfs, two funny sheep, the familiar Hippo and for the first time the little elephant, which we know from the "Resonance" sand picture (Picture 1) are placed in the sand. All of them have dishes in front of them and "nourish the cell," Pia commented.

While she was shaping this picture, Pia told me that indeed muscular dystrophy is the result of an inability of the muscle cells to absorb a specific substance. She also said that she knew very well that by symbolically feeding her cells, her muscles were still not cured. But her soul felt healed and happy, because feeding her body meant for her to accept it and to care for it. She also said with great joy that for the first time she felt a oneness within herself and no longer a painful split between her psyche and her body.

Then she explained to me that over the many years she had worked in the sand tray, the images she had created always nourished her soul and helped her to balance her inner pain. Furthermore, she said that the sand pictures had helped her to develop positive feelings for herself, and that through the images, she learned how to nourish herself. She expressed that through creating the sand pictures she had created for herself an inner foundation of images which then, from within, stimulated her ability to act out in the world. These images, she said, gave her the energy to go on in life and also gave her the profound certainty that her life was precious even though her body was not perfect.

I understood that now Pia had reached a new equilibrium, and that her psyche had become reconciled with her body.

In the next session, she created the picture of "Resonance" (Picture 1). It shows in a beautiful way how her body (the monkey) is contained in the field of the heart, in the field of love, between the little elephant as a symbol for Pia and the big elephant as a symbol for myself.

I still would like to reflect on this question: "What is it, that is hidden in the 'old' big elephant, which represents my part of the analytical resonance?"

I believe that first of all it is my basic attitude towards my work: I keep in mind the pathology of my clients, but I do not emphasize it. I am mainly – it's my nature – in resonance with my client's healthy potential, with the parts that can be developed.

And I love my work, especially as a sandplay therapist. I am never bored with my clients, I love to watch their inventiveness and creativity. I find it interesting to observe even the smallest signs of something growing out of the sand or the smallest sign of change and renewal.

So it is certainly my basic attitude to be open for new and creative aspects of my clients' development. I am not afraid of chaos or dissolution, because I learned early in my life that any renewal or new construction is preceded by a deconstruction. De-construction means to take things apart, re-construction means to join them again, and a creative reconstruction means to join the parts in a new and meaningful way. That is sandplay! Compose an image in the sand and later decompose it – compose the sand in a new and unexpected way and again decompose it. Through this ongoing, subtle movement of composing and decomposing, sand picture after sand picture, finally a significantly renewed personality gets born.

Once a sand picture is finished, I let my clients talk about it. I gently invite them to tell me their view of it. If I see an aspect in the picture differently – not if I *interpret* the picture differently! – or if I see something that my client did not see, I may just mention it. Thus, my contribution of seeing a picture and my client's way of seeing it become superimposed. The two views begin to intermingle and very often, over time, a dissonance of experiences, understanding or noticing something changes into a positive resonance. The interaction becomes almost a partnership, it is, so to speak, like weaving together an image or like composing a piece of music together.

In conclusion, I would say that in sandplay therapy (or in analysis) the phenomena of projection, of transference and countertransference are embraced or embedded in the larger and more holistic principle of analytical resonance. This resonance is, although a very intimate one, never only related to two individual persons. It is related to what happens in the hermetic vessel of the sand tray. Out of the resonance between two persons grows "The Third One," which touches and changes both of them. The music of two instruments playing together is greater than the sum of the two parts. It is new, unique music. It's not predictable, in music or in psychotherapy, there is always a mystery – a mysterium – to discover!

Of course, all this is true not only for therapists and clients, analysts and analysands, but also for teachers and pupils, doctors and patients, parents and children and many other human relationships where, through the phenomenon of resonance, one person creates for the other one the basic condition for growth, development and new life.

Thus, resonance has to do with Eros, with a field of loving relationship, which, in Pia's beautiful last sand picture, is represented by the heart.

References

1 For example: Ammann, Ruth (1987), *Das Traumbild Haus*. Düsseldorf: Walter.
  Ammann, Ruth (1999), "Innenraum und Aussenraum, Lebensräume der Menschen, gesehen mit einem architektonischen Auge und einem psychologischen Auge", in *Lebensräume, Spielräume, Schutzräume*. Düsseldorf: Walter.
2 Ammann, Ruth (2001), Chapter 11, "The case of Anna suffering a phobia of red", in *Das Sandspiel, Der schöpferische Weg der Persönlichkeitsentwicklung*. Düsseldorf: Walter.
3 Jung, C.G. (1993), *Memories, Dreams, Reflections*, recorded and edited by Aniela Jaffé. London: Fontana Press, p. 253.
4 Hahn, Peter (2001), *Das Geheimnis therapeutischer Wirkung*. Heidelberg: Carl-Auer-Systeme.
5 Cramer, Friedrich (1998), *Symphonie des Lebendigen. Versuch einer allgemeinen Resonanztheorie*. Frankfurt: Insel Taschenbuch.
6 Bach, Susan (1990), *Life Paints Its Own Span*. Einsiedeln: Daimon.

Susan Bach

Life paints its own Span

The pioneering work, *Life Paints Its Own Span*, with over 200 color reproductions, is a comprehensive exposition of Susan Bach's original approach to the physical and psychospiritual evaluation of spontaneous paintings and drawings by severely ill patients. At the same time, this work is a moving record of Susan Bach's own journey of discovery.

SUSAN BACH
LIFE PAINTS ITS OWN SPAN

On the Significance
of Spontaneous Pictures by
Severely Ill Children

Part I (Text): 208 pages
Part II (Pictures): 56 pages
ISBN 3-85630-516-5

Ann Belford Ulanov
Spiritual Aspects
of
Clinical Work

Ann Belford Ulanov

Spiritual Aspects of Clinical Work

How does the spirit come into clinical work? Through the analyst? In the analysand's work in the analysis? What happens to human destructiveness if we embrace a vision of non-violence? Do dreams open us to spiritual life? What is the difference between repetition compulsion and ritual? How does religion feed terrorism? What happens if analysts must wrestle with hate in themselves? Do psychotherapy and spirituality compete, or contradict, or converse with each other? What does religion uniquely offer, beyond what psychoanalysis can do, to our surviving and thriving? This book is chock full of such important questions and discussions of their answers.

476 pages, ISBN 3-85630-634-X

English Titles from Daimon

Available from your bookstore or from our distributors:

In the United States:

Bookworld Trade Inc.
1941 Whitfield Park Loop
Sarasota FL 34243
Please order on the web: www.bookworld.com
Fax: 800-777-2525 Phone: 800-444-2524

In Great Britain:

Airlift Book Company
8 The Arena
Enfield, Middlesex EN3 7NJ
Phone: (0181) 804 0400
Fax: (0181) 804 0044

Worldwide:

Daimon Verlag   Hauptstrasse 85   CH-8840 Einsiedeln   Switzerland
Phone: (41)(55) 412 2266   Fax: (41)(55) 412 2231
email: info@daimon.ch

Visit our website: www.daimon.ch
or write for our complete catalog